ENHANCED
ETHNOGRAPHIC
METHODS

ETHNOGRAPHER'S TOOLKIT

Edited by Jean J. Schensul, *Institute for Community Research, Hartford,* and
Margaret D. LeCompte, *School of Education, University of Colorado, Boulder*

The **Ethnographer's Toolkit** is designed with you, the novice fieldworker, in mind. In a series of seven brief books, the editors and authors of the **Toolkit** take you through the multiple, complex steps of doing ethnographic research in simple, reader-friendly language. Case studies, checklists, key points to remember, and additional resources to consult are all included to help the reader fully understand the ethnographic process. Eschewing a step-by-step formula approach, the authors are able to explain the complicated tasks and relationships that occur in the field in clear, helpful ways. Research designs, data collection techniques, analytical strategies, research collaborations, and an array of uses for ethnographic work in policy, programming, and practice are described in the volumes. The **Toolkit** is the perfect starting point for professionals in diverse professional fields including social welfare, education, health, economic development, and the arts, as well as for advanced students and experienced researchers unfamiliar with the demands of conducting good ethnography.

Summer 1999/7 volumes/paperback boxed set/0-7619-9042-9

BOOKS IN THE ETHNOGRAPHER'S TOOLKIT

1. **Designing and Conducting Ethnographic Research,** by Margaret D. LeCompte and Jean J. Schensul, 0-7619-8975-7 (paperback)

2. **Essential Ethnographic Methods: Observations, Interviews, and Questionnaires,** by Stephen L. Schensul, Jean J. Schensul, and Margaret D. LeCompte, 0-7619-9144-1 (paperback)

3. **Enhanced Ethnographic Methods: Audiovisual Techniques, Focused Group Interviews, and Elicitation Techniques,** by Jean J. Schensul, Margaret D. LeCompte, Bonnie K. Nastasi, and Stephen P. Borgatti, 0-7619-9129-8 (paperback)

4. **Mapping Social Networks, Spatial Data, and Hidden Populations,** by Jean J. Schensul, Margaret D. LeCompte, Robert T. Trotter II, Ellen K. Cromley, and Merrill Singer, 0-7619-9112-3 (paperback)

5. **Analyzing and Interpreting Ethnographic Data,** by Margaret D. LeCompte and Jean J. Schensul, 0-7619-8974-9 (paperback)

6. **Researcher Roles and Research Partnerships,** by Margaret D. LeCompte, Jean J. Schensul, Margaret R. Weeks, and Merrill Singer, 0-7619-8973-0 (paperback)

7. **Using Ethnographic Data: Interventions, Public Programming, and Public Policy,** by Jean J. Schensul, Margaret D. LeCompte, G. Alfred Hess, Jr., Bonnie K. Nastasi, Marlene J. Berg, Lynne Williamson, Jeremy Brecher, and Ruth Glasser, 0-7619-8972-2 (paperback)

ENHANCED ETHNOGRAPHIC METHODS

Audiovisual
Techniques,
Focused Group
Interviews,
and Elicitation
Techniques

JEAN J. SCHENSUL
MARGARET D. LeCOMPTE
BONNIE K. NASTASI
STEPHEN P. BORGATTI

3 ETHNOGRAPHER'S TOOLKIT

A Division of Sage Publications, Inc.
Walnut Creek • London • New Delhi

Copyright © 1999 by Altamira Press, A Division of Sage Publications, Inc.

All rights reserved. No part of this book may be reproduced or utilized in any form or by any means, electronic or mechanical, including photocopying, recording, or by any information storage and retrieval system, without permission in writing from the publisher.

For information:

AltaMira Press
A Division of Sage Publications, Inc.
1630 North Main Street, Suite 367
Walnut Creek, CA 94596
explore@altamira.sagepub.com
E-mail: http://www.altamirapress.com

SAGE Publications Ltd.
6 Bonhill Street
London EC2A 4PU
United Kingdom

SAGE Publications India Pvt. Ltd.
M-32 Market
Greater Kailash I
New Delhi 110 048 India

Printed in the United States of America

Library of Congress Cataloging-in-Publication Data

Schensul, Jean J.
    Enhanced ethnographic methods: Audiovisual techniques, focused
group interviews, and elicitation techniques / Jean J. Schensul,
Margaret D. LeCompte, Bonnie K. Natasi, and Stephen P. Borgatti:
        p.   cm. — (Ethnographer's toolkit; v. 3)
    Includes bibliographical references and index.
    ISBN 0-7619-9129-8 (pbk.: alk. paper)
    1. Ethnology—Methodology. 2. Ethnology—Research.
3. Ethnology—Audio-visual aids. 4. Focused group interviewing.
I. LeCompte, Margaret Diane. II. Nastasi, Bonnie K. III. Borgatti,
Stephen P. IV. Title. V. Series.
    GN345.S36   1999
    305.8′001—ddc21   98-40071

This book is printed on acid-free paper.

99 00 01 02 03 04 05 10 9 8 7 6 5 4 3 2 1

Production Editor: Astrid Virding
Editorial Assistant: Denise Santoyo
Designer/Typesetter: Janelle LeMaster
Cover Designer: Ravi Balasuriya
Cover Artists: Ed Johnetta Miller, Graciela Quiñones Rodriguez

CONTENTS

INTRODUCTION

The **Ethnographer's Toolkit** is a series of texts on how to plan, design, carry out, and use the results of applied ethnographic research. Ethnography, as an approach to research, may be unfamiliar to people accustomed to more traditional forms of research, but we believe that applied ethnography will prove not only congenial but essential to many researchers and practitioners. Many kinds of evaluative or investigative questions that arise in the course of program planning and implementation cannot really be answered very well with standard research methods such as experiments or collection of quantifiable data. Often, there are no data yet to quantify or programs whose effectiveness needs to be assessed! Sometimes, the research problem to be addressed has not yet been clearly identified and must be discovered. In such cases, ethnographic research provides a valid and important way to find out what *is* happening in programs and to help practitioners plan their activities.

This book series defines what ethnographic research is, when it should be used, and how it can be used to identify and solve complex social problems, especially those not readily amenable to traditional quantitative or experimental research methods alone. It is designed for educators; service professionals; professors of applied students in the fields of teaching, social and health services, communications, engineering, and business; and students working in applied field settings.

Ethnography is a peculiarly human endeavor; many of its practitioners have commented that, unlike other approaches to research, the *researcher* is the primary tool for collecting primary data. That is, as Books 1, 2, 3, and 4 demonstrate, the ethnographer's principal database is amassed in the course of human interaction: direct observation; face-to-face interviewing and elicitation; audiovisual recording; and mapping the networks, times, and places in which human interactions occur. Thus, as Book 6 makes clear, the personal characteristics and activities of researchers as human beings and as scientists become salient in ways not applicable in research, where the investigator can maintain more distance from the people and phenomena under study.

Book 1 of the **Ethnographer's Toolkit**, titled *Designing and Conducting Ethnographic Research,* defines what ethnographic research is and identifies the predominant viewpoints or paradigms that guide ethnography. It provides the reader with an overview of research methods and design, including how to develop research questions, what to consider in setting up the mechanics of a research project, and how to devise a sampling plan. Ways of collecting and analyzing data, as well as ethical considerations for which ethnographers must account, conclude this overall introduction to the series. In Book 2 of the **Ethnographer's Toolkit**, titled *Essential Ethnographic Methods,* readers are provided with an introduction to participant and nonparticipant observation, interviewing, and ethnographically informed survey research, including systematically administered structured interviews and questionnaires. These data collection strategies are fundamental to good ethnographic research. The essential methods provide ethnographers with tools to answer the principal ethnographic questions: "What's happening in this setting?" "Who is engaging in what kind of activities?" and "Why are they doing what they are doing?" Ethnographers use them to enter a field situation and obtain basic information about social structure, social events, cultural patterns, and the meanings people give to these patterns. The essential tools also permit ethnographers to learn about new situations from the perspective of "insiders" because they require ethnographers to become involved in the local cultural setting and to acquire their experience through hands-on experience.

In Book 3, *Enhanced Ethnographic Methods,* the reader adds to this basic inventory of ethnographic tools three different but important approaches to data collection, each one a complement to the essential methods presented in Book 2. These tools are audiovisual techniques, focused group interviews, and elicitation techniques. We have termed these data collection strategies "enhanced ethnographic methods" because each of them parallels and enhances a strategy first presented in Book 2.

Audiovisual techniques, which involve recording behavior and speech using electronic equipment, expand the capacity of ethnographers to observe and listen by creating a more complete and permanent record of events and speech. Focused group interviews permit ethnographers to interview more than one person at a time. Elicitation techniques allow ethnographers to quantify qualitative or perceptual data on how individuals and groups of people think about and organize perceptions of their cultural world.

It is important for the reader to recognize that, whereas the essential ethnographic methods described in Book 2 can be used alone, the enhanced ethnographic methods covered in Book 3 cannot, by themselves, provide a fully rounded picture of cultural life in a community, organization, work group, school, or other setting. Instead, they must be used in combination with the essential methods outlined in Book 2. Doing so adds dimensions of depth and accuracy to the cultural portrait constructed by the ethnographer.

In Book 4, *Mapping Social Networks, Spatial Data, and Hidden Populations,* we add to the enhanced methods of data collection and analysis used by ethnographers. However, the approach taken in Book 4 is informed by a somewhat different perspective on the way social life is organized in communities. Whereas the previous books focus primarily on ways of understanding cultural patterns and the interactions of individuals and groups in cultural settings, Book 4 focuses on how social networks and patterns of interaction, as well as uses of what we term "sociogeographic space," influence human behavior and beliefs.

Book 5, *Analyzing and Interpreting Ethnographic Data,* provides the reader with a variety of methods for transforming piles of fieldnotes, observations, audio- and videotapes, questionnaires, surveys, documents, maps, and other kinds of data into research results that help people to understand their world more fully and facilitate problem solving. Addressing narrative and qualitative, as well as quantitative —or enumerated—data, Book 5 discusses methods for organizing, retrieving, rendering manageable, and interpreting the data collected in ethnographic research.

In Book 6, *Researcher Roles and Research Partnerships,* we discuss the special requirements that doing ethnographic research imposes on its practitioners. Throughout the **Toolkit,** we have argued that there is little difference between the exercise of ethnography as a systematic and scientific enterprise and applied ethnography as that same systematic and scientific enterprise used specifically for helping people identify and solve human problems. To that end, in Chapter 1, "Researcher Roles," we first describe how the work of ethnographers is inextricably tied to the type of person the ethnographer is, the particular social and cultural context of the research site, and the tasks and responsibilities that ethnographers assume in the field.

In the second chapter, "Building Research Partnerships," we recognize that ethnography seldom is done by lone researchers. We discuss how ethnographers assemble research teams, establish partnerships with individuals and institutions in the field, and work collaboratively with a wide range of people and organizations to solve mutually identified problems. The chapter concludes with ethical and procedural considerations including developing social and man-agerial infrastructure, establishing and breaking contracts, negotiating different organizational cultures and values, and resolving conflicts.

Book 7, *Using Ethnographic Data,* consists of three chapters that present general guidelines and case studies illustrating how ethnographers have used ethnographic data in planning public programs, developing and evaluating interventions, and influencing public policy.

Throughout the series, authors give examples drawn from their own work and the work of their associates. These examples and case studies present ways in which ethnographers have coped with the kinds of problems and dilemmas found in the field—and described in the series—in the course of their work and over extended periods of time.

Readers less familiar with ethnographic research will gain an introduction to basic ethnographic principles, methods, and techniques by reading Books 1, 2, 5, and 6 first, followed by other books that explore more specialized areas of research and use. Those familiar with basic ethnographic methods will find Books 3, 4, and 7 valuable in enhancing their repertoires of research methods, data collection techniques, and ways of approaching the use of ethnographic data in policy and program settings.

In this book, Chapter 1, titled "Audiovisual Methods in Ethnography," covers audiovisual data collection techniques, including audiotaping and video recording. Recording audio and visual data requires ethnographers to consider what they want to record and how to frame and focus the camera—or, what to look at or listen to. Audiovisual recording can fall victim to equipment failure and the unwillingness of research participants to be recorded. Notwithstanding, audiovisual recording can improve the quality of data collection and analysis because it can create a more complete record of observation, which permits the ethnographer to replay events—to view them or listen to them—repeatedly so as to do more accurate analysis and interpretation. Audio- and videotapes also permit viewing by a number of analysts, helping to generate multiple—and therefore more complete—interpretations of events. In this chapter, readers will learn when to record and how to make decisions on what to record. Equipment needs as well as ways to transcribe and code audio- and videotapes also are reviewed. The author ends with some creative suggestions for how to use audiovisually recorded data for a variety of purposes.

Chapter 2, titled "Focused Group Interviews," defines group interviews, both formal and informal, and discusses the circumstances under which they are most useful. Simply put, focused group interviews are a structured approach to interviewing people in groups. Group interviews often occur naturally in field settings. The reader will learn how to take advantage of moments in which group interviews can be arranged spontaneously to capture the interaction of group members on a particular topic. More formal group interviews, or focused groups, can be used to speed the process of individualized interviewing or to reveal patterns of communication or differences of opinion that might not emerge in a collection of individual interviews. Chapter 2 details the skills and organizational considerations needed to conduct good formal group interviews, including how to frame questions, reduce barriers to information collection, avoid logistical problems, attend to the ethical considerations that can arise in a group discussion, and manage and use focused group data. The reader also is cautioned about the limitations of data obtained from focused groups; like other forms of interviewing, focused group interviews are more useful for telling us how group members think than they are for revealing specifically what people do.

The third chapter, "Elicitation Techniques for Cultural Domain Analysis," introduces the reader to strategies for capturing the ways that people organize their thinking about culture and cultural components. In this chapter, readers will be introduced to the three most important techniques for discovering domains and subdomains of culture: listings, pilesorts, and triad sorts. Listings are one of the most important ways to discover cultural domains and subdomains. Pilesorts are used to obtain data on the way a group of respondents organizes items, ideas, or things within a cultural domain. Pilesorting ultimately forces a group to agree on the organization of cultural domains so that the result is a "best fit" picture of the group's cognitive map of, or way of structuring, their cultural domain. Triad sorts use similar strategies; both triad sorts and pilesorts require participants to make comparisons (for sameness) and contrasts (for differences) among items, ideas, or things.

Each of these elicitation techniques provides ways to quantify qualitative data on the way people organize their perceptions of objects and behavior in their cultural environments. These techniques help researchers to understand how people structure these perceptions in cultural domains or areas of culture, determine how such domains are related to each other, and discover to what extent groups of people differ in their ways of thinking about and organizing culture.

—Jean J. Schensul and Margaret D. LeCompte

1 ❈━❈━•━❖

AUDIOVISUAL METHODS IN ETHNOGRAPHY

Bonnie K. Nastasi

INTRODUCTION

I like to do things that boys do. I would like to be a boy some-times. If you climb a tree you cannot because you cannot do that and be ladylike. I cannot eat a lot. It is not ladylike. I don't shout. Girls are brought up to be polite. Boys are more free. You cannot go to a friend's house like to spend a day or a night. Boys can. They can come home late and they won't get scolded or beaten. Parents have old ideas. Parents say, "We were brought up like this, so you will do this." If we go higher in education, they say a woman should stay at home and cook. We don't agree with that. (Comments from adolescent girls in a developing country during a group interview; Nastasi, Varjas, Sarkar & Jayasena, 1998)

Through interviews such as this one, ethnographers are able to capture people's thoughts and feelings in their own language. Such data provide important insights into individual experiences and cultural practices. Traditionally, ethnographers have relied on the written record to capture informants' responses or to note their observations in natural contexts. Audiovisual techniques—consisting of audiotaping and videotaping—provide an alternative or supplement to the extensive written record that is the hall-mark of traditional ethnography.

1

The focus of this chapter is the use of audiovisual techniques to study human development or behavior in natural settings, such as classrooms or communities, in contrast to the traditional application of these techniques in controlled clinical or laboratory research settings. Audiovisual technology is particularly advantageous for collecting certain types of observational and interview data, such as observing human interaction or conducting group interviews. One primary advantage is the permanent and complete record of observations or dialogue, which can be used for analysis and interpretation of data. Although not completely free of researcher bias, audiovisual recording provides a record of events that can be readily subjected to interpretation by different researchers and from multiple perspectives.

The chapter provides you the opportunity to consider several critical issues related to the use of audiovisual technology in ethnographic research: What is the focus of your research? How can audiovisual technology be used to answer your research question(s)? What logistical decisions need to be made about the use of audiovisual technology? How should you approach transcribing, coding, and interpretation of recorded data? How can the audiovisual record be used to enhance data interpretation and facilitate the integration of research and practice? We examine each of these issues, drawing from research in psychology, education, and anthropology that has been conducted by Nastasi and her colleagues.

CONCEPTUAL CONSIDERATIONS

The first consideration in any research project involves conceptual issues related to the focus of your research (i.e., your research questions) and the philosophical or theoretical basis of your research questions. As we explore later in the chapter, your questions and the underlying perspectives influence how you approach the process of data collection, transcribing, coding, and interpretation. For example, whether you begin with specific research questions (derived from existing theory, research, and/or your own applied experiences) or prefer to investigate in an inductive manner (allowing theory to evolve from your data) has critical implications for the entire research process.

Research Questions to Focus Audiovisual Data Collection

- What is the subject matter?
- Where can it be found?
- What behaviors or interactions do you want to record?
- When should you record?
- What period of time is sufficient (i.e., how frequently should you record)?
- How long should each session last?
- Should recording be continuous or intermittent?
- Whom should you record?

Before you begin to record, you must answer several questions about the focus of your research: *What is the subject matter* (e.g., students' interactions during cooperative learning, as they work in dyads/pairs or small groups)? *Where can it be found* (in a classroom in which the teacher uses cooperative learning)? *What behaviors or interactions do you want to record* (student-student interactions, teacher-student interactions, or both)? *When should you record* (e.g., only when students are interacting in groups, or for the entire class period)? *What period of time is sufficient? That is, how frequently should you record* (daily or weekly; for one semester or the entire school year)? *How long should each session last* (30 minutes or the full class period)? *Should recording be continuous* (for the duration of the 55-minute class session) *or intermittent* (at random 10-minute intervals)? *Whom should you record* (all students within the classroom or selected pairs or groups of students; one classroom or several; one grade level or several)? The experiences of one group of researchers illustrates how these questions are considered in a classroom context.

EXAMPLE 1.1

CONCEPTUAL AND LOGISTICAL CONSIDERATIONS IN A CLASSROOM CONTEXT

In a study of fifth graders' interactions during cooperative learning, the researchers (reports are found in Nastasi, Johnson, & Owens, 1995; Nastasi & Young, 1994; Young, Nastasi, & Braunhardt, 1996) considered several conceptual and logistical issues: Is our focus or conceptual attention on the interaction between individual students as they work in pairs/dyads within the classroom? If so, we do not need to videotape whole-class instructional activities unless we are interested in how whole-class instruction is related to the dyad work (e.g., Does the teacher provide instructions on how to work together?). Also, are we interested in what else is occurring in the classroom as we focus on a specific dyad? If so, we need multiple recorders to capture the simultaneous occurrences. However, there is the issue of equipment resources. Do we have or can we purchase multiple cameras and microphones? And would multiple cameras be more disruptive to the classroom? Other critical conceptual questions included the following: Are we more interested in an in-depth study of a few select students, or do we want a wider sample across all students within the classroom? Do we want to examine continuous interactions over time, or are periodic samples of interactions sufficient? Alternatively, if we want a record of ongoing classroom interactions and do not want to make decisions about sampling of the interactions beforehand, we could simply do continuous recording of the natural sequence of events and then sample after recording is finished. The answers to these questions, of course, depend in part on our resources. For example, do we have enough recording equipment and personnel to do continuous recording and/or simultaneous recording of different dyads? And could we use audiotape recorders for some dyads and videotapes for others? What is most important to capture— students' discussion or actions or both?

◆●◆●◆

Key point　　As the preceding example demonstrates, *the researchers' decisions are influenced by multiple considerations.* It is advisable to start with the conceptual issues, determining what kind of data are essential to answer your research questions, and then consider what is feasible given available resources. The following description provides an example of how the combination of conceptual and logistical considerations influenced decisions about audiovisual recording in an applied research project.

EXAMPLE 1.2

CONCEPTUAL AND LOGISTICAL CONSIDERATIONS IN A COMMUNITY CONTEXT

The purpose of the research project was to develop, implement, and evaluate an intervention for adolescent girls and their mothers to reduce the risk of substance abuse. The intervention was conducted in small groups in three formats: girls only, mothers only, and girls and mothers mixed. The intervention program required that group facilitators or leaders (i.e., staff members who were responsible for implementing the intervention) use certain facilitation strategies (e.g., questioning, prompting, modeling) for presenting information, encouraging group discussion, and engaging the group members in solving real-life dilemmas collaboratively (e.g., How do I respond to peer pressure to drink alcohol?). Data collection was necessary to document the use of facilitation strategies by group leaders in order to ensure program integrity (i.e., Is the program being carried out as specified?) and identify needs for additional staff training. Furthermore, researchers were interested in examining the extent to which the facilitation strategies promoted certain participant behaviors (e.g., considering different approaches to solving dilemmas).

Continuous recording of all sessions during a pilot study permitted in-depth study of the intervention process. There were sufficient personnel, cameras, and videotapes to record all sessions. However, human resources were insufficient for transcription and coding all of the tapes. Thus, the decision was to videotape all sessions so that a full documentation was available as archival data. This permitted the use of tapes for multiple purposes: documenting implementation, assessing facilitators' skills, and examining the relationships between facilitator strategies and participant behaviors. Furthermore, comprehensive recording during the pilot phase could help researchers make informed decisions about recording during the subsequent intervention project (Schensul, Berg, & Romero, 1997).

Once conceptual questions are answered, researchers face a series of methodological decisions related to recording, transcribing, coding, and interpretation and use of data. Some of the decisions that researchers must make apply to collection and analysis of ethnographic data in general (e.g., coding), but others (e.g., taping) are specific to the use of audiovisual techniques. Additionally, issues may vary depending on which type of recording—audio or video—the researchers choose to use. We begin with logistical considerations.

LOGISTICS

> ### Logistical Considerations
>
> - Videotape versus audiotape
> - Should fieldnotes be used?
> - Research staff needed and/or available?
> - Acquiring and using audiovisual equipment and supplies
> - The influence of recording on the natural setting
> - Resources necessary in the setting to ensure that the equipment will function
> - Recorders
> - Confidentiality

Traditionally, the ethnographer need only equip himself or herself with a notebook to record fieldnotes, observations, dialogue, and so on. When using audiovisual techniques, however, the ethnographer is faced with a number of decisions: Should you audiotape or videotape? Should you also collect fieldnotes? What are the staff requirements? What needs to be considered as you purchase and use equipment and supplies? In addition, using audiovisual recording technology in natural settings requires certain considerations not relevant to contrived or laboratory settings, where these techniques traditionally have been used. For example, to what extent does the recording equipment (particularly, video cameras) alter the natural setting? What resources are necessary within the natural context (i.e., is electricity necessary)? Who will do the recording? How can confidentiality or anonymity be preserved when using recording devices? How do you effectively capture specific interactions in uncontrolled settings, for example, where background noise is a potential problem (e.g., how do you record a conversation between two individuals in a room full of people)? We address these and other questions as we explore the major logistical issues.

Audiotaping Versus Videotaping

One critical decision is whether to do audiotaping or videotaping. When one has a choice, videotaping usually is preferable because it provides a broader array of behavioral data. Specifically, videotapes permit the consideration of nonverbal behaviors in interpretation of individual or interactive responses. Nonverbal behaviors can facilitate interpretation of interview as well as observational data. For example, in individual interviews, the addition of nonverbal cues permits one to better interpret the respondents' responses (e.g., through facial cues or eye contact with the interviewer). In dyadic (pairs) or group interviews, videotapes can facilitate the identification of individual speakers and examination of group dynamics. Additionally, videotapes provide data on physical contextual variables, such as spatial arrangement, lighting, objects, and artifacts. Finally, *the continuous videotaped record can foster understanding of the complexity of a situation or the sequence of actions or events.* **Key point**

Videotaping, however, does have disadvantages. Equipment is more expensive. Greater attention to the recording equipment is necessary (e.g., to ensure that the camera stays in focus). The equipment is more visible and thus can be more intrusive; that is, people tend to be more aware of being filmed than of being audiotaped. Additionally, maintaining anonymity of respondents is more difficult with videotapes because they are visually identifiable. This is particularly important when informants are minors; are physically, mentally, or culturally vulnerable; are in some type of custody arrangement; or are providing sensitive information. These situations do not prevent the use of videotapes, but researchers must take extra precautions to protect access to the tapes. Perhaps most importantly, *the videotape transcription process is much more complex and time consuming than it is for audiotapes, particularly if you are interested in analyzing nonverbal behaviors and physical environment features.*

Key point

Notetaking

Another consideration is whether some form of notetaking is necessary in addition to audiovisual recording. As a general rule, audio/videotaping does not replace fieldnotes as a method of recording the ethnographer's impressions and capturing more global aspects of the context. It is possible to record notes and impressions on audio/video-tape at the beginning and end of a taping session, but it also is necessary to take written notes during a session. The need to accompany audio/videotapes with fieldnotes also depends on the context. For example, the researcher may find the tapes sufficient when the entire context is easily captured on videotape, the session is of relatively short duration, and comments and impressions can be recorded easily on tape at the end of the session. [There are, of course, situations when notetaking during a session is not feasible; for example, when your attention is directed toward conducting an interview or focus group. In such cases, addi-

Cross Reference: See Chapter 2 on recording and notetaking in focus groups

tional staff might be necessary to gather written notes.] The following example illustrates the use of fieldnotes to supplement videotape data.

 **EXAMPLE 1.3**

USING FIELDNOTES TO SUPPLEMENT VIDEOTAPE DATA

In one study conducted in a fifth-grade classroom, researchers used videotaping to record whole-class, dyadic (pairs of students), and small-group activities. The purpose of the study was to examine the nature of students' interactions with each other as they engaged in cooperative learning over several months. However, researchers found it necessary to take fieldnotes in addition to taping in order to capture the more global aspects of the classroom context. For example, ethnographers took written notes about (a) global physical features such as arrangement of desks (drawing a map of the classroom), bulletin boards, rules posted in the classroom; (b) activities outside of the camera's range, for example, as students left their desks to seek help from the teacher or use reference materials (e.g., a central computer); and (c) the global instructional context, such as teachers' instructions to the whole class and the activities of students outside of the target dyad or small group. The ethnographers' record of informal conversations with teachers provided critical data about the teachers' perspective. Furthermore, the ethnographers recorded their impressions garnered from observations; these impressions were invaluable to subsequent data analysis and interpretation (Nastasi et al., 1995; Nastasi & Young, 1994; Young et al., 1996).

As suggested in the preceding example, the complexity of natural contexts such as classrooms or community settings present challenges for researchers who are using audiovisual recording. Without multiple cameras, it is impossible to capture permanent records of the multiple activities and events occurring simultaneously. In such situations, fieldnotes are essential to understanding contextual factors. In addition, the ethnographers' fieldnotes provide invaluable data about their own impressions during observations.

Audiovisual technology also can be used to supplement written records or fieldnotes. That is, audio/videotaping can be conducted to provide a backup or archival record to the ethnographer's written records. The following description illustrates such use and further exemplifies the complementary nature of fieldnotes and tapes as permanent records.

EXAMPLE 1.4

USING AUDIOVISUAL TECHNOLOGY TO SUPPLEMENT FIELDNOTES

In one study, researchers conducted focus groups with adolescents attending schools in a community in Sri Lanka. The purpose of the study was to understand mental health issues among Sri Lankan youth in order to inform the development of culturally specific, school-based mental health programs. The groups were conducted by American and Sri Lankan co-researchers. The Sri Lankan researcher also served as interpreter. Two research assistants, one Sri Lankan and one American, were present to record verbalizations in the primary native language (Sinhala) and English, respectively. The translation process and the timing of interchanges permitted the research assistants to document all dialogue in both languages. In addition, discussions were audiotaped. The written transcripts in English served as the database for coding. The notes taken in Sinhala were used to supplement the English notes, provide another perspective on interpretation of Sinhala responses, and provide culturally specific terminology for key constructs. The research assistants also recorded contextual features and nonverbal behaviors. The on-site notetaking permitted identification of different speakers, which would have been difficult with audiotapes alone, given the group structure and language differences. The tapes were used to verify written notes when ambiguities arose, and they provided an archive of the interviews in two languages (Nastasi, Varjas, Sarkar, & Jayasena, 1998).

Research Staff

Given the multiple tasks required in conducting audiovisual recording, another critical consideration involves staff. Who will perform the multiple tasks necessary for recording? As noted in the previous section, it may not be feasible for one person to conduct a session (e.g., interviewer), monitor the recording equipment, and take written notes. Alternatively, you might consider hiring a research team, consisting of one or more interviewers, technicians to handle the audiovisual equipment, and notetakers. In the applied research study described earlier, Schensul and her colleagues hired different staff members for the multiple tasks. During a session, one person facilitated the intervention (group facilitator), another monitored the videocamera (filmer), and a third took fieldnotes (notetaker). Such division of labor facilitated accurate and comprehensive recording (Schensul et al., 1997).

Acquiring and Using Audiovisual Equipment and Supplies

A critical set of decisions involve the selection, purchase, and use of audiovisual equipment and supplies. Following are listed recommendations to assist you in making these decisions. These suggestions are based on extensive experience with audiovisual recording for research purposes. Given that your database is the audio or video record, careful selection and use of equipment and supplies are essential. Costs of equipment and supplies should be considered as you plan your study. In this section, we discuss each of the recommendations.

> *Tips for Selecting, Purchasing, and Using
> Audiovisual Equipment and Supplies*
>
> ■ Acquire professional audiotaping or videotaping equipment designed for commercial use.
> ■ Purchase good quality microphones that meet your specific needs.
> ■ Purchase good quality audiotapes or videotapes.
> ■ Purchase a good tripod for positioning the camera.
> ■ Test and monitor your equipment regularly.
> ■ Use appropriately trained personnel for recording.
> ■ Mark all tapes clearly.
> ■ Make backup copies of all tapes and store originals in a safe, secure place.

Key point   *Acquire high-quality professional audiotaping or videotaping equipment designed for commercial use.* Researchers should purchase the best equipment possible, preferably of professional production quality. Personal (retail) recording and playback equipment, although less expensive, provides fewer options (e.g., less control over viewing speed and playback capabilities). Consider your needs with regard to research purposes, context, and logistics. In selecting equipment, portability is likely to be an issue. For example, can the camera remain stationary in the research site, or do you need something that is easily moved about? Consider whether battery-operated recording equipment (camera, microphone, audio-recorder) is needed, and inquire about the cost and feasibility of extended use of battery-operated equipment. Consider whether videocameras permit recording of date and time directly on the tape.

Another critical consideration is the degree to which the equipment allows flexibility for reviewing tapes. Transcription equipment is available for facilitating the review of audiotapes by providing greater control of the rewinding and pausing functions than is possible with typical audio-taping machines (e.g., the transcription machine has foot-pedal control so that your hands can remain on the key-board). Make sure that playback equipment (audio or video) permits ease of repeated playback and pausing (e.g., you are returned to the exact location after a pause), mul-tiple speeds for reviewing tapes, a counter that provides a time record, and minimal slippage (e.g., you want to be able to return to the exact spot on a tape as indicated by the counter—for repeated viewing and for intercoder agree-ment purposes). Headsets also are available to permit pri-vate review of audiotapes or audio portions of videotapes. Software programs are available that permit connections between video playback equipment and computer, so that the computer controls the playback equipment (e.g., Video-Toolkit™, 1992). Such software facilitates the coordination of viewing and transcribing. It is important to inquire about the feasibility of connections between your computer and the video playback equipment as you purchase equipment; and to consider the availability, cost, and ease of use of the software as well as the compatibility of the software require-ments with your existing computer.

Purchase good quality microphones that meet your specific **Key point**
needs. There are a variety of microphones from which to choose, and they vary in utility, convenience, and price. It is very important to know whether the microphones built into cameras and audio-recorders are sufficient for your purposes. The built-in microphones are frequently inade-quate for capturing vocalizations of specific individuals in group settings (e.g., focus groups or group interventions) or for recording target conversations in settings with back-ground noise (e.g., recording a student-teacher conversa-tion in classroom) or when target individuals are moving about (e.g., teacher in a classroom). In these situations,

alternatives are necessary that permit focused recording and minimize recording of background noise (when using either audio or video equipment). For both audio and video recording, PZM (flat) microphones, which can be placed on a flat surface (e.g., table around which a group is seated), are ideal for capturing target conversations while minimizing background noise. PZM microphones are relatively inexpensive. Clip-on microphones are the best alternative for capturing vocalizations of target individuals (e.g., the teacher in the classroom or individuals within a group). Wireless clip-on microphones are particularly useful in situations in which the target individual is moving about (e.g., a teacher who moves about the classroom). The cost of wireless clip-on microphones, however, may be prohibitive. It is important to investigate such costs as you plan the project budget.

 Key point *Purchase good quality audiotapes or videotapes.* Generally, tapes of shorter duration are better. For repeated reviewing, tapes of 60 to 90 minutes are preferable to those of longer length because the tape quality is more likely to be maintained. Also, it is easier to find segments efficiently. Particularly when doing continuous recording, 90-minute tapes are preferable to 60-minute tapes because you need to change the tape less often.

 Key point *Purchase a good tripod and position the camera securely.* If you intend to place the camera in a stationary position for video recording, it is important that you purchase a good tripod. Particularly in high-activity situations, the camera must be secure. In all situations, it is critical to designate someone to be responsible for monitoring the recording equipment to ensure accurate focus of the camera and continual recording.

Test and monitor your equipment regularly. Before every session, make sure both video and audio functions work. If you are using battery-operated equipment, make sure batteries are still operative. Always carry additional batteries. Between sessions, recharge batteries if applicable. Monitor taping throughout the session. Although more convenient, letting the recorder or camera run unattended is risky. Valuable data can be lost if your equipment fails, the tape runs out, or the target activity or people move out of video or audio range.

Key point

Use appropriately trained personnel for recording. This is particularly critical when doing videotaping. Make sure camera personnel know how to operate equipment. If the camera will not remain in a stationary position, make sure the person responsible for the camera can record effectively while moving about. Limit the number of people who are responsible for taping. When multiple recorders must be used, make sure the guidelines for taping are clearly articulated and consistently implemented. Otherwise, the quality of recordings may vary widely, and you may lose critical data. The best recorders are familiar with the use of the tape recorder or camera, and they are well informed about the study, the scientific or other reasons for recording, and what they should be recording.

Key point

Mark all tapes clearly. Record dates and identifying information about participants and situation on each tape, either on labels or directly on the audio or video record. Record critical identifying information about participants and situation on the audio and/or visual portions of your tape. Properly label all tapes. Trying to discern the context of an unmarked taped session can be frustrating and result in loss of data, particularly as time passes.

Key point

Key point   *Make backup copies of all tapes, and store the originals in a safe and secure place.* You should make backup copies of tapes to prevent the loss of original data. Repeated viewing can lessen the quality of the recording. Tapes can be misplaced. It is impossible to recover data if tapes are damaged or lost. If several individuals will be viewing or coding tapes, make multiple backups. Store the original tapes in a safe and secure place (e.g., locked cabinet in your office). Make sure tapes are properly labeled. Protect tapes from extremes of temperature, dust, and magnetic sources. Use appropriate precautions for protecting the confidentiality and anonymity of taped respondents.

Key point   In summary, *research questions and logistical considerations (e.g., the number of cameras or tape recorders, the number of data collectors, the extent of resources for transcribing and coding of tapes) influence decisions about procedures for data collection.* As a general rule, more extensive recording (audiotaping or videotaping) provides the greatest flexibility for data analysis and interpretation; that is, researchers have the luxury of reviewing and reanalyzing archival records. An extensive sample of recorded observations permits subsequent return to the original data to explore other interpretations and, most importantly, to understand the phenomena under study within the real-life context. Finally, the use of audio/videotaping does not preclude the need for fieldnotes about one's impressions, informal interactions, and global features of the environment.

Definition: Transcription is the process of transforming audio portions of tapes to written form and adding written descriptions of interaction and setting.

TRANSCRIPTION

Transcription is critical in accessing data for analysis because much analysis is conducted on textual data. However, coding or analysis also can be conducted directly from the taped record. Although this section is focused on approaches to transcribing data into textual format, we address the issue of direct coding from audio- or videotapes as well.

Transcription can be approached in a number of ways. It varies along a continuum from full transcription of all verbal and nonverbal behaviors and contextual factors to a summary of critical incidents. The approach you choose depends on the nature of the data you need as well as feasibility of transcription in terms of time and cost. For example, full transcription provides a thorough description of all verbalizations and, in the case of videotapes, nonverbal behaviors and physical context. However, it is time consuming and tedious. In this section, we examine the use of full transcription and transcribing of selected segments. We conclude with consideration of alternatives to transcribing, such as coding directly from tapes.

Full Transcription

Transcribing entire audiotapes or videotapes is a labor-intensive and time-intensive endeavor, but it yields a level of detail that permits close and repeated analysis of the data. In using this approach, it is necessary to review sections of the tape repeatedly in order to capture both verbal and non-verbal behaviors, as well as physical contextual features. This transcription technique precedes any attempts to code data. With such a thorough documentation, it is possible to code directly from the transcripts and to use the transcripts repeatedly to address alternative questions. To ensure accuracy, it is necessary to have a second transcriber review the tapes and fill in gaps that might have been left by the first transcriber. Even though transcribing is straightforward, some level of interpretation is needed. Thus, a second transcriber can also provide a reliability check. Alternatively, once tapes have been transcribed and are ready for coding, the coder can serve as a second transcriber, filling in the gaps or raising questions about differences in interpretation of actions or vocalizations. It is much more difficult to do a full transcription of videotapes than of audiotapes. Whereas full transcription of audiotapes requires only detailed recording of all verbalizations, full transcription of videotapes requires description of both verbal and nonverbal behaviors (e.g., vocalizations, body language, facial expressions). The following excerpts exemplify the level of detail required in transcribing audio and video representations.

Video examples. The following transcribed segments are from a videotaped session in which two third-grade girls are working collaboratively at a computer (Nastasi & Clements, 1992). The excerpts depict both verbal and nonverbal behavior (nonverbal behavior is noted in parentheses) as the students create a computer graphics program. At this point, they are trying to create letters for a display. Student 1 is typing, and Student 2 is seated beside her. FD20 is a command that moves the pointer on the screen "forward 20 spaces." Students use the protractor to assist them in creating angles. In the first segment, the level of detail helps to create a picture of the student's actions and reactions to the products of her work.

EXAMPLE 1.5

FULL TRANSCRIPTION OF ONE STUDENT'S
BEHAVIOR AS SHE WORKS AT A COMPUTER

Student 1:   (types, looks at the screen) Okay. (typing) FD20. (looking at the screen) Wait a minute. (taking the protractor and measuring the design on the screen) Oh, deary me, deary me, deary me. (types, looks at the screen, types, looks at the screen) Oh god, this is difficult (types, looks at the screen, types, looks at the screen) Now what do I do? (clapping her hands and leaning back in her chair) I know what, no I don't (looking at the screen, then at Student 2). What are you writing?

➤•➤•➤

EXAMPLE 1.6

FULL VIDEO TRANSCRIPTION OF TWO STUDENTS' INTERACTIONS
AS THEY WORK TOGETHER AT ONE COMPUTER

This excerpt is from the same session as in Example 1.5.

Student 1: (pointing to the folder) Write FD20 down.

Student 2: How come you make me do all the work? (reaching for the pencil)

Student 1: Yeah, 'cause I have to do this (typing). 10. Where's the protractor? (looking at Student 2)

Student 2: You have your own. (getting out of her seat)

Student 1: No I don't, I only have my folder (looked toward the camera, then looks toward the door, holding on to the cabinet with her left hand, balancing the chair on the two left legs) Au-uh-uh! (looks at Student 2, takes the protractor from Student 2 and puts it on the screen, making noises with her mouth)

Student 2: (out of view) There, now I'm erasing.

Student 1: (types, looks at the screen, types, looks at the screen) Yes! Ooh! (sitting back, then forward, types, looks at the screen, types, then looks at the screen, then reaches for the protractor, making noises with her mouth while measuring the design on the screen, types, looks at the screen) Ooh ma-ma, ooh ma-ma. (dancing in her seat, making silly noise, then looking at Student 2) [Name], what are you doing?

Student 2: I'm writing a procedure.

Student 1: Oh, okay, while I do this? (looks at the screens, then types)

Student 2: That way I'll have the procedure done.

Student 1: (types, looks at the screen, types, looks at the screen) I got the "M" done. (jumping back, looks at Student 2, hands on keyboard, positioned to type) Wait a minute. Go ask [the teacher] if I want to do an "E," how do I get to an "E"? (looking at Student 2, tapping her feet on the floor)

Audio example. The following excerpt is from an interview with two fifth-grade girls about their understanding of cooperative learning (Nastasi et al., 1995; Nastasi & Young, 1994; Young et al., 1996). The two students have been working daily for several weeks as partners (a dyad) on a problem-solving project in mathematics class. These students had agreed to be interviewed on a weekly basis about their work in mathematics class.

EXAMPLE 1.7

FULL AUDIO TRANSCRIPTION OF INTERVIEW WITH TWO STUDENTS

Interviewer: What do you think are the qualities of a good problem-solving dyad or team?

Student 1: Umm.

Student 2: Cooperation.

Interviewer: Okay.

Student 1: Well, understanding each other's point, like trying to see the other person's point and not just staying with your idea.

Interviewer: Mm-hmm.

Student 1: Like, be flexible. Don't always have to go with, like . . .

Student 2: Whatever you came up with and you stay there, and you never know.

Interviewer: Mm-hmm.

Student 1: Yeah.

Interviewer: Okay. Anything else you can think of?

Student 1: Getting along.

Interviewer: Okay. What, what do you mean by that? In terms of, like, cooperating and getting along?

Student 1: Getting along. Like, um, sort of trying to work together.

Interviewer: Okay.

Student 1: Like, staying together and working together. Don't go off and do something yourself.

Interviewer: Mm-hmm.

Student 1: Like, you know, think sort of positively, like, you know, we're partners. We're supposed to be together.

Interviewer: Mm-hmm.

Student 1: And even if we don't, like, if our teacher matched us up, and like, um, I got with my worst friend, and [Student 2] got with her worst friend, and we didn't all, we wa-. Like, say we wanted to be partners really bad, and we didn't get each other as partners, and you know, we would still have to work cooperatively and try to understand other people's, and you know, not be a brat to the other person.

Interviewer: Mm-hmm. W-what do you mean by being a brat?

Student 1: Like, you know, always saying the wrong, like, um, telling them, arguing over stuff, like who's gonna get to write, who's gonna get to use the computer.

Interviewer: Mm-hmm.

Student 1: And, you know, just arguing over stupid things that don't really matter.

Student 2: I know.

Student 1: Like, you know, "you took my pencil," and things like that.

Whether transcribing audiotapes or videotapes, it is criti- **Key point**
cal to select an experienced transcriber who is familiar with
the focus of your work. For example, the transcriber must
be familiar with the nature of the research and the level of
detail that is necessary. It is likely that the first time you work
with a transcriber, you will need to review the transcriptions
to ensure that the transcription is accurate and the level of
detail of nonverbal behaviors and/or vocalizations is sufficient. If you do not have time and resources for a full
transcription, you may opt to use more economical alternatives, such as transcribing selected segments of tapes.

Transcribing Selected Segments

> *Approaches to Selecting*
> *Segments for Transcription*
>
> ■ Sample the tapes
> ■ Select relevant segments
> ■ Identify and fully transcribe critical incidents; summarize
>   rest of content

In lieu of transcribing entire tapes, you may choose to
transcribe segments of the audio/videotapes. There are
three possible approaches to selecting segments.

Sample the tapes. The first approach is to purposefully or
randomly select segments of the tapes to yield a sample of
data across time, contexts, and participants. Thus, you
might identify critical variables (e.g., level of expertise in
problem solving) and then purposefully select within those
constraints (e.g., choose a novice and an expert problem
solver). Or, to obtain a representative sample of variations
across key variables (e.g., problem solvers with different
skill levels), you might randomly select segments across all
videotaped sessions.

Select relevant segments. The second approach is to transcribe only segments of the tape that are relevant to the research question. For example, if you are studying cooperative learning and are interested primarily in the quality of exchanges between students as they work together, transcription could be restricted to cooperative interactions between students. The remainder of the tapes could be summarized to provide an indication of the larger context; for example, the transcriber could summarize other activities of the class session (e.g., whole-class instruction, individual seatwork) during which the cooperative student interactions (e.g., students working in small groups) occur. This second approach requires that the transcriber be knowledgeable enough of the focus of the research to identify tape segments that need full transcription versus summarizing.

Definition: Critical incidents are recorded events that exemplify a code

Identify critical incidents. The third approach is to identify **critical incidents** that exemplify the codes, and transcribe fully the critical incidents while also summarizing the context. That is, the transcriber must first identify the incident (e.g., disagreement between individuals) that exemplifies the code (e.g., idea conflict) and then transcribe it fully.

EXAMPLE 1.8

TRANSCRIPTION OF A VIDEOTAPED CRITICAL INCIDENT

In one study, Nastasi and her colleagues were interested in conflict resolution strategies within dyadic (pairwise) interactions; that is, in how fifth-grade students working collaboratively resolved their disagreements. The following excerpts depict examples of *cognitive (idea) conflict* (i.e., partners disagree about how to solve a problem) with two different types of conflict resolution: *resolution by teacher* (i.e., teacher intervenes to resolve the conflict) and *resolution by negotiation* (i.e., partners discuss the discrepant ideas and agree on mutually agreeable problem solution by compromise or acceptance of one of the proposed ideas). The rule for transcribing was that the transcription had to be detailed enough to justify the target code (e.g., idea conflict with resolution) and distinguish it from alternative codes (e.g., distinguish the levels of resolution):

Idea Conflict With Resolution by Teacher

(Both girls then continue reading or repeating numbers from the [computer] monitor.)
Student 1: (reading from the monitor) Number of the line you wish to save . . . 1.
Student 2: No, you want to save 2.
Student 1: What?
Student 2: You want to save 2.
Student 1: (turns to the teacher) Do we want to save 2?
Teacher: No, you want to save that line you're on right there.

(Student 2 appears confused about which one, asks which line the teacher means, and the teacher says it should be line 2.)
Students 1 & 2: (simultaneously) Oh!

Idea Conflict With Resolution by Negotiation

(Both girls then read the next question, "How long are the barges?")
Student 1: Uh oh.
Student 2: 200.
Student 1: Okay, 200 feet each. . . .
Student 2: No, 200 feet altogether.
Student 1: No, but . . . there was three barges, and they were 200 feet each, remember?
Student 2: Oh yeah!
Student 1: Let's put 200 feet.

SOURCES: Nastasi et al., 1995; Nastasi & Young, 1994; Young et al., 1996.

The critical incident approach to transcribing requires the skills of a transcriber-coder, because the coding and transcribing processes are closely linked. That is, transcribers must be well-trained, experienced coders who are experts in the use of the specific coding scheme. In addition, effective use of this method requires the use of unambiguous guidelines for application of the coding scheme. Thus, extensive practice in use of the scheme with the specific data set is necessary before transcribing can proceed.

Alternatives to Transcribing

Key point   *Transcription is not always necessary.* For example, when using event-recording (e.g., how frequently did the event occur) or time-sampling (e.g., for what time period did the behaviors occur) procedures, coding can be done directly from videotapes or audiotapes without first transcribing. (Coding is addressed in a subsequent section.) In such instances, the coder views (or listens to) the tape and records either the occurrence or time engaged in target behaviors or events. This technique is useful if the researcher is interested only in representing the data in terms of frequency or time and is unconcerned with the degree to which incidents of the behavior or activity vary qualitatively. Additionally, the target constructs must be easily defined as discrete, observable behaviors (or discrete verbalizations). As the following example illustrates, nonverbal conflict is more easily documented by a frequency count than is verbal conflict.

EXAMPLE 1.9   ⬤▬⬤▬⬤

FEASIBILITY OF FREQUENCY COUNT OF VERBAL VERSUS NONVERBAL CONFLICT

In a study of students' interactions during partner work at a computer, researchers Bonnie Nastasi and Doug Clements were interested in both nonverbal and verbal conflicts between students. An example of *nonverbal conflict* is one student grabbing the keyboard while the other is typing. An example of *verbal conflict* is disagreement about how students should share resources and responsibilities (e.g., discussing what should be typed and who should type). "Grabbing the keyboard" from one's partner is a discrete behavior that is easily distinguished and counted. In this study, researchers were not interested in how students "grab" materials from their partners; they were interested only in occurrences of such behaviors. "Disagreements," in contrast, could involve a brief interchange about sharing the keyboard, as follows:

Student 1: I want to type now.
Student 2: You have already typed for most of the class [session].
Student 1: Okay, you can type for the rest of today.

Alternatively, "disagreements" could involve lengthy discussions about how to complete an assignment, as follows:

Student 1: The teacher says we need to decide on the steps [for a computer program] and then enter them onto the computer [type in the commands]. So, let's decide how we want to do this.
Student 2: Well, I think we should start by choosing all the steps and writing them down. Then we can take turns typing in the commands.
Student 1: No, I think we should just decide and type as we go. You tell me what to do and I'll type.
Student 2: But that is not what the teacher told us to do. And besides, I want to type first. [The discussion continued.]

Verbal conflicts (disagreements) were less easily represented as discrete events than were nonverbal conflicts (grabbing). Furthermore, the researchers were interested in the nature of the disagreements; that is, what kind of arguments were posed and how the disagreements were resolved. As reflected in the preceding interchanges, the students approached resolution of the disagreement differently. Thus, transcriptions of verbal disagreements were critical. Recording frequency or duration (how many times disagreements occurred, or how long discussions over disagreements lasted) was insufficient for understanding how students worked together (Nastasi & Clements, 1992).

CODING

The coding process involves (a) the selection/development of a coding scheme, (b) training coders and providing practice in applying the coding scheme, and (c) implementing procedures to ensure consistent application and interpretation of the scheme by establishing and maintaining intercoder agreement.

Selecting/Developing a Coding Scheme

The selection and/or development of a coding scheme can range from the adoption of a preexisting scheme to the inductive development of a unique scheme. We examine three variations along this continuum.

Adopting a preexisting coding scheme. At one extreme, the researcher selects a scheme that has been developed by other researchers investigating similar phenomena or is based on the researcher's earlier work. This most likely occurs when extensive theoretical and empirical work has been conducted on the phenomenon under study in the same or similar contexts, as the following case example illustrates.

➤●➤●➤

Coding Scheme

Case Study: Researchers Nastasi and Clements developed a coding scheme to study patterns of collaboration as individuals work in pairs (dyads) or small groups to solve mathematical or social problems. The following section addresses conflicts between or among individuals and strategies for resolving the conflicts.

Cognitive or idea conflict. Two or more individuals engage in a conflict of ideas or disagreement about task conceptualization or solution. Partners present different ideas and make explicit their recognition of a disagreement. For example, students present differing ideas about how to solve an assigned problem and acknowledge that their ideas are different.

Social conflict. Verbal or nonverbal behavior of individuals indicates a discrepancy in expectations about the social aspect of the interaction. For example, partners state that their expectations about sharing resources differ ("I thought I could use the calculator first"), or they engage in behavior such as criticizing others, name calling, or hitting.

Conflict Resolution Strategies

No resolution. Conflict remains unresolved.

Teacher resolution. Teacher intervenes and resolves the conflict.

Social dominance. The solution is socially imposed by one partner and/or the other partners acquiesce.

Social negotiation. Partners resolve the conflict through mutual negotiation on a purely social basis (e.g., "We used your idea last time, so this time we use my idea").

Idea dominance. Resolution is imposed by one partner but with consideration of the quality of the ideas that were proposed. That is, one or more partners provide a logical rationale for the proposed solution(s) before resolution is reached. However, the selected solution is imposed by one partner and/or the other partner(s) acquiesce.

Idea negotiation. Resolution is reached through a mutual agreement of partners, typically following discussion of the merits of alternative perspectives. Agreement can reflect the decision to accept one of the proposed ideas or a compromise between opposing positions.

Idea synthesis. Resolution reflects a synthesis of opposing viewpoints. That is, the final resolution is an integration of different ideas into a qualitatively different solution.

The scheme was initially developed to study the interactions of children in preschool and kindergarten classrooms (Nastasi & Clements, 1994). The researchers used the scheme in a number of studies with school-age children ranging from Grades 1 through 6 (Clements & Nastasi, 1988; Nastasi & Clements, 1992; Nastasi, Clements, & Battista, 1990). They modified the codes and created new codes to permit more detailed examination of conflicts (e.g., distinguishing social from cognitive conflicts) and resolution strategies (delineating several strategies for conflict resolution) across a variety of populations and contexts. The process of modification of the scheme was based on research findings that linked certain interactions (resolution of cognitive conflicts through negotiation) with desired outcomes (higher-order thinking skills in intervention studies; e.g., Nastasi & Clements, 1992). Furthermore, the use of the scheme by different coders and with different collaborators forced revisions of the codes to facilitate understanding. That is, as different research partners questioned the meaning of specific codes, researchers refined definitions to ensure clarity.

This coding scheme has been used most recently to guide training and conduct process evaluation in risk prevention research with adolescents and adults. In this research, group facilitators were trained to present cognitive conflicts (dilemmas depicting risky situations) to small groups of participants (e.g., six to eight members) and to encourage group members to discuss the dilemmas and generate solutions through negotiation of different viewpoints (alternative approaches to solving the dilemma). In addition, researchers investigated the interactions among group members as they discussed dilemmas to determine how the discussion process contributed to expected outcomes (enhanced decision-making skills). Furthermore, in one study, the definitions of conflict resolution strategies were used to facilitate self-evaluation of group dynamics. That is, group members were given descriptions of the resolution strategies and asked to identify the strategies they used to resolve disagreements in their groups (Nastasi et al., in press; Schensul et al., 1997).

━●━●━

Modifying a preexisting scheme. An alternative to adopting a preexisting scheme is to modify the preexisting scheme to fit the phenomenon and context under study. This is likely to occur when some early theoretical and databased work has been conducted, but the scheme is not general enough to be applicable across all populations and contexts. Given both the individual and contextual variation of most human phenomena and the nature of ethnography, most preexisting schemes will require at least some modification. What is essential is that the researcher identify the appropriate definition and interpretation of codes for the specific focus of the inquiry. Usually, through the course of a research program, an individual researcher or team of researchers develops a general framework for coding with flexibility for application to specific individuals and/or contexts, as illustrated in the preceding example. As Nastasi and her colleagues applied the scheme to different contexts, the

coding scheme was modified to examine new research questions. The following provides an illustration.

EXAMPLE 1.10

MODIFYING A CODING SCHEME

In earlier versions of the scheme (Nastasi & Clements, 1992), the teacher's presence with the target pair or group was coded as "noncollaborative" activity, and "collaborative" activity was restricted to the times when students were working together without teacher assistance or intervention. As these researchers investigated the interactions of student pairs (dyads) over a period of time (e.g., the school year), they became interested in the role of the teacher in facilitating collaboration among students (e.g., when students asked the teacher for help, or when the teacher intervened with specific groups in the process of monitoring their work; Nastasi, Bingham, & Clements, 1993). At this point, the coding scheme was modified to incorporate teacher presence. Thus, instances of collaboration when the teacher was interacting with the group were distinguished from those when the teacher was not involved directly with the group. This change in coding scheme permitted in-depth study of the teacher's influence on the nature of students' collaboration (Nastasi et al., 1995).

Developing a new coding scheme. Another alternative is the inductive development of a unique coding scheme. This is most likely to occur in the theory development process, when relatively little is known about the phenomenon of interest or when the target population or context is totally unfamiliar. With an inductive or grounded theory approach, the coding categories originate or evolve from the data. In such instances, the ethnographer/researcher sets out to define the phenomenon of interest purely from the perspective of those being studied (i.e., from the "emic" perspective). In contrast, when the researcher applies a preexisting scheme without modification, the phenomenon is interpreted from the perspective of the researcher (i.e., from the "etic" perspective).

The researcher's approach to developing a new scheme may vary in terms of the influence of existing theory and research. For example, in the early stage of theory development, the researcher may approach the data in a highly inductive manner, with a minimum of preconceived ideas. In this situation, the researcher starts the process of scheme development by reviewing all of the recorded or transcribed data and identifying relevant categories for classifying behaviors, ideas, events, and so on. These categories then become the basis for coding the data; that is, coders apply the code to the full set of data. Subsequent refinement of the coding scheme might involve identification of subordinate or superordinate categories to most appropriately represent the data and explain the phenomenon under study. The following is an example of this process.

Cross Reference: See Book 5, Chapter 5, for a discussion of how codes emerge from data

EXAMPLE 1.11

INDUCTIVE DEVELOPMENT OF A CODING SCHEME

In a study of sexual risk among youth in Sri Lanka, sociologist Tudor Silva, anthropologist Stephen Schensul, and their colleagues conducted extensive, in-depth interviews with young male and female adults. These informants were questioned about sexual knowledge, attitudes, and practices (in addition to other aspects of their lives). Transcripts of the interviews were reviewed, and any reference to "sex" was identified. One particular category of interest was sexual behaviors. Little was known about sexual practices in this culture, and prior research had shown cultural variations in the sequence of sexual behaviors (e.g., ranging from holding hands to sexual intercourse).

The research team, through careful examination of the data, identified a series of "heterosexual" behaviors relevant to the Sri Lankan culture. Some behaviors involved several variations, thus yielding subordinate categories. In addition, the researchers, through further study of this young adult population, were able to categorize the behaviors in terms of types of sexual risks (e.g., shame, pregnancy, loss of virginity) and level of sexual risk (e.g., ranging from no or minimal risk to high risk for sexually transmitted diseases [STDs]). This categorization scheme provided an important framework for understanding sexual risk, directing further study within this and other cultures, and informing the development of risk-prevention interventions for youth (Silva et al., 1997).

━●━●━●━

Training Coders

> ### Guidelines for Preparing Coders
>
> ■ Inform coders about ethical issues
> ■ Provide an introduction to the research
> ■ Make sure coders understand research methods and concepts in the study

How the researcher develops a coding scheme influences the training or preparation of coders as well as the establishment of intercoder agreement (which we examine in the next section). In this section, we examine training of coders with regard to adopting or modifying a preexisting scheme or developing a new scheme.

Regardless of the approach to coding, there are a few general guidelines for preparing coders. First, researchers must inform coders about ethical issues, such as the need to maintain security of data and to protect the identity of informants. Second, they should provide an introduction to the purpose and methodology of the research. Third, they must make sure coders have an appropriate level of knowledge about research methodology and the conceptual basis of the work.

Adopting a preexisting scheme. If you select a preexisting scheme, training of coders is straightforward. The researcher provides:

■ The coding scheme with predetermined categories and definitions
■ Examples of earlier applications of the scheme
■ Practice in applying the codes to subsets of the new data set or similar data sets
■ Feedback on the accuracy of application

The sequence of instruction, demonstration, practice, and feedback continues until coders have reached an appropriate level of precision in terms of accuracy, consistency of application, and agreement with other coders on the use of the scheme. This sequence would be followed, for example, in using the Nastasi and Clements (1994) scheme presented in an earlier section.

Steps in Modifying or Creating a Coding System

- Coders learn about the research, its theoretical base, and the local culture
- Researcher and coders develop and assign codes based on transcripts
- Coders work individually
- Researcher and coders compare and discuss codes
- Coding system is refined
- Coders become full partners in the coding process
- Coders teach new coders

Modifying a preexisting scheme. With modification of an existing scheme, training of coders becomes a more participatory process. The coders are provided information about the existing scheme, the assumptions underlying the scheme, and the focus of the current work. Then, coders participate collaboratively with the researcher in application and modification of the existing scheme by going through the following steps.

First, the researcher and coders together review transcripts and discuss assignment of codes to the text. In this phase, the focus of discussion is on the meaning of codes, distinctions among codes, and boundaries of categories (i.e., what meaning is central to the category, what is peripheral, what is outside of the category—what fits, what does not). The lead researcher and coders then start to develop exemplars of the coding categories for future reference. This phase continues until there is sufficient clarity to permit coders to work independently.

Next, the coders work individually with sample transcripts and convene with the researcher to compare and discuss coding. In this phase, the same transcript segments are chosen for coding by all coders. The researcher and coders then meet and compare the application of categories across coders, identify points of agreement, and discuss discrepancies in coding. The focus, again, is on clarification of meaning and identification of category boundaries and exemplars. Researchers and coders agree on new codes, collapsing or expanding existing coding categories, and the creation of new subcategories. The purpose is to develop a coding scheme that fits the questions, population, and context of the specific study. In addition, the coding team is developing consistent application and interpretation of the coding scheme, progressing toward intercoder agreement. This process is guided initially by the researcher.

With practice, the coders become full participants in the process. If the process works well, members of the coding team develop enough expertise to work independently of the researcher. At this point, the researcher meets periodically with coders to monitor consistency of application, as well as serves as a consultant for coders to resolve discrepancies and/or discuss further modifications of the scheme. Coders should develop sufficient expertise to teach new coders.

The potential outcome of collaboration between the primary researcher and coders can be beneficial. It was in the context of discussing coding that the researchers Nastasi and Clements, and the coder-collaborator (Bingham, a doctoral student in anthropology) raised questions about the difference between dyadic (2 students) and triadic (2 students with teacher) interactions. In particular, the active presence of the teacher could serve to disrupt or facilitate collaborative activity, depending on whether the teacher provided direct instruction or prompted students to consult with each other, respectively. In this instance, the collaborative process resulted not only in revision of the scheme, but also in the generation of new research questions (Nastasi et al., 1993).

Developing a new coding scheme. When using an inductive process to develop a coding scheme, coders again become full participants or co-researchers. The process of preparing coders and developing the scheme is similar to that just described for modification of existing schemes.

 Key point *For coders to participate as collaborators in generating and applying the coding scheme, they must become familiar with the underpinnings of the work, particularly the purpose of the research, the researcher's theoretical-empirical base and related work, and the culture being studied.*

The coders then familiarize themselves with the data by reviewing transcripts and related documents. The coders, in collaboration with the researcher(s), generate categories for organizing the data. For example, researcher and coders (research-coding team) individually review data, suggest organizing schemes, and then meet to compare and discuss schemes. Through a process of consensus building, the research-coding team generates a scheme to be applied to the transcripts. The process of application and refinement is similar to that described earlier. The research-coding team independently code selected transcripts, meet to discuss and clarify the meaning and boundaries of codes, and modify the scheme as needed. Eventually, the coders reach a level of expertise that permits independence, seeking consultation with the researcher as needed. The researcher continues to monitor the process for consistency among coders and across the data.

Coders as co-researchers. The following illustrates the involvement of coders as co-researchers. In this project, coders not only participated in coding interviews but also contributed to the inductive process of identifying key constructs for understanding mental health among Sri Lankan youth.

EXAMPLE 1.12

CODERS AS CORESEARCHERS

Initially, the existing theory and research about mental health in Western cultures guided the investigation of mental health needs and resources in Sri Lanka. Several key constructs (e.g., competencies, stressors, coping strategies) were used to develop interview questions for students and school staff in an urban community in Sri Lanka, and they were subsequently used to guide the initial coding of interview transcripts. The initial coding process served to segment the data into broad categories (key constructs), from which culture-specific categories/codes were inductively derived. The coders, who were doctoral students in psychology, assisted in the initial coding process as well as the process of subsequently generating a culture-specific scheme for depicting the mental health of Sri Lankan youth. To participate effectively in these processes, the students/coders needed to become familiar with both the relevant literature on mental health and Sri Lankan culture (Nastasi et al., 1998).

In summary, the preparation of coders varies as a function of one's approach to selecting and developing a coding scheme. At one extreme, coders are trained in the use of a preexisting scheme. It is the researcher's responsibility to make sure they learn to apply the scheme in a consistent and accurate manner. At the other extreme, coders are full participants in the inductive development of a coding scheme. In the latter case, they become co-researchers. How you approach the selection or development of a coding scheme and the preparation of coders depends on your approach to inquiry. In my own experience, coders who develop a deep understanding of the research focus and process generate trustworthy (reliable and valid) data and develop ownership

Key point   in the research process. *Thus, preparing expert coders goes well beyond teaching them to use the coding scheme in a consistent manner. It requires educating them about the research focus and process so that they become co-researchers.*

Ensuring Consistency in Coding:
Intercoder Agreement

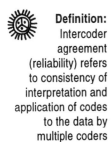

Definition: Intercoder agreement (reliability) refers to consistency of interpretation and application of codes to the data by multiple coders

Intercoder agreement (also termed interrater agreement or reliability) refers to the consistent interpretation and application of codes to the data set by multiple coders. Initially, a common understanding must be established between/among prospective coders. Subsequently, consistency checks across individual and multiple coders must be conducted throughout the process of coding. If the researcher is using an existing coding scheme, the process of establishing intercoder agreement involves teaching coders to use the scheme in a consistent manner. Although application of the scheme to different contexts and individuals or groups may require some modification of the definitions of codes or categories, it is typically expected that such changes will be minimal. Thus, the focus is on establishing a consistent interpretation and application of preexisting codes.

If the coding scheme is being developed in an inductive manner, then the process of establishing intercoder agreement involves the construction of categories and their definitions. Coders are more active in constructing the meaning of codes, and establishing intercoder agreement becomes more of a collaborative process among coders/researchers. Of course, even in an inductive approach, the primary researcher can identify and define all codes and then teach coders to interpret and apply codes consistently to the data.

With either of the aforementioned options, establishing agreement is best accomplished through guided practice in applying the scheme, followed by independent practice in coding by every coder, with checks for consistency. When inconsistencies occur, discussion regarding discrepancies in interpretation is needed. Such discussions may yield clarification of meaning of the codes or redefinition of codes. In some instances, discussions will result in development of new coding categories representing different constructs or in elaboration of existing constructs. The process of independent coding with discussion continues until an acceptable level of agreement is reached. Depending on the complexity of the coding scheme and the level of involvement of coders in modifying or developing the scheme, this process can take a considerable amount of time. For example, the application of the scheme developed by Nastasi and Clements (1994) to a new context with new coders can take several months. The process, however, typically involves modification of code definitions or creation of new codes, as has been described in an earlier section.

Traditionally, intercoder (interrater) agreement involves the computation of a quantitative index of agreement, which represents the percentage of agreement between or among coders; that is, the frequency of agreement in the application of specific codes to a particular data segment. An acceptable starting point is at 85% to 90% agreement (for more detailed discussion, see Bakeman & Gottman, 1986). Alternatively, a more subjective index may be used; that is, comparison continues until discrepancies in application are no longer apparent to the coders. Any discrepancies are minor and can be resolved easily through discussion. It is critical that agreement be established prior to final application of the coding scheme. If this is not done, when new codes or new interpretations arise halfway through the coding process, coders will need to review and recode tapes or transcripts that have already been completed. The critical issue here is consistency across coders and over the sample of data.

Consistency checks should be done periodically throughout the coding process to protect against "observer drift," that is, the tendency for observers/coders to change their interpretations or definitions of codes over time. The researcher must ensure that changes in application and/or interpretation of codes reflect "real" changes in the phenomenon being studied. For example, if the nature of collaborative learning among peers changes as a function of an intervention (e.g., the contributions of peers become more equal following a training session on sharing responsibilities), then the definition of the construct should reflect this change. In such a case, the "collaborative learning" code might still be applied, but the qualitative change with respect to equitability of contribution needs to be described in the interpretation of data. Or, a new subcode might be added to reflect level of contribution of peers. Alternatively, the coders might redefine their definition, independent of the natural phenomenon (e.g., after one or more coders read research on collaborative learning). Once the coding system has been finalized, this form of redefinition is unacceptable because it reflects a change in the coders' interpretation of the "same" (similar) phenomenon.

INTERPRETATION

The researcher's approach to data interpretation is influenced by the conceptual focus of the study and the approach to data analysis. The meaning that the researcher attributes to data is influenced by the extent to which the researcher has relied on existing theory and research to frame research questions and guide coding. If the researcher approached both data collection (e.g., interview questions) and the coding of data with a specific focus, framed within existing theory and research, it is likely that the same focus or framework will influence the interpretation of the data as well. For example, if the researcher adopts a preexisting scheme for coding data, it is likely that the scheme also will guide data interpretation, as illustrated by the following.

EXAMPLE 1.13

DATA INTERPRETATION USING A PREEXISTING CODING SCHEME

Suppose a group of researchers decides to adopt the coding scheme developed by Nastasi and Clements (1994). They code interactions of students working in small groups for instances of cognitive or idea conflict, social conflict, and resolution strategies. The data are summarized to show the number of idea and social conflicts, as well as the proportion of conflicts (idea and social) that are resolved using each of the resolution strategies. That is, the researchers (a) describe the students' interactions in terms of the number of idea versus social conflicts and how those conflicts were resolved, (b) compare how groups varied with regard to frequency of conflicts and resolution strategies, and (c) attempt to explain the learning of individual students in terms of their experience with conflict and resolution during group work. The researchers conclude with a discussion of the extent to which their findings confirm or disconfirm existing theory and research.

Alternatively, researchers approach data collection and coding in a more inductive manner, with the goal of building theory rather than adopting existing theory. Thus, the research questions and initial coding categories are broad in focus, and a more specific coding scheme is derived from the data. We return to the work of Silva et al. (1997) to illustrate this process.

EXAMPLE 1.14

DATA INTERPRETATION WHEN CODE CATEGORIES ARE INDUCTIVELY DERIVED

As noted earlier, Silva and his colleagues identified a unique sequence of heterosexual behaviors relevant to the sexual practices of young adults in Sri Lanka on the basis of the descriptions provided by representatives of this population. They also identified types of sexual risk that these young adults considered to be important; these risks defined sexual risk for this population (i.e., sexual risk included loss of virginity, loss of relationships, social stigma, pregnancy, sexually transmitted diseases [STDs] and HIV/AIDS). Finally, researchers identified the respondents' perceptions about the link between specific behaviors and specific sexual risks. The researchers then used this information to create a culture-specific risk-prevention program (Nastasi et al., in press). That is, the intervention focused on promoting accurate perceptions of risk by helping participants to link culture-specific patterns of sexual behavior to various types of risk. These perceptions then guided decision making aimed at risk reduction.

━●━●━●━

USE OF AUDIOVISUAL DATA[1]

> *Uses of Audiovisual Data*
>
> ■ Facilitate interpretation through
> — Researchers' repeated reviews of tapes
> — Participants' reviews of tapes to inform researchers
> — Participants' reviews for own self-reflection
> — Presentation and discussion of findings
> ■ Foster integration of research and practice

The ethnographic data generated from audiovisual technology have multiple uses, some of which are unique to the audiovisual record. As we noted at the beginning of this chapter, ethnographers are interested in capturing behaviors, thoughts, feelings, and products that provide insights into cultural phenomena in order to better understand human behavior within the context of culture and (in the case of applied ethnography) to design interventions to effect individual and/or cultural change. Data derived through the use of audiovisual technology can be applied easily to the same interpretative and applied purposes.

Using Audiovisual Data to Facilitate Interpretation

Audiovisual data can be used to facilitate or enhance interpretation in a number of ways. As we noted earlier, the

permanent audiovisual record provides unlimited opportunities to review, reanalyze, and reinterpret data. Tapes also
afford the opportunity for researchers to review the data in
context. Analysis and interpretation of data transcribed
from videotapes are greatly enhanced by viewing relevant
segments of the tape. Even with very detailed transcriptions
that include verbalizations, actions, and contextual descriptions, the tapes provide a visual supplement for charac-
terizing context, events, and so on. The videotape facilitates
the creation of a "mental picture," or gestalt, of the events.
In addition, review of tapes helps the viewer to put critical
incidents into context so that they are not interpreted as
isolated events.

Second, audiovisual records provide a unique medium
for presenting data to participants to enhance the researcher's analysis and interpretation of data and ensure
that the participants' perspectives are reflected accurately.
Similarly, the audiovisual record can be used to foster collaboration between researchers and participants; that is,
participants collaborate in data analysis and interpretation
and thus become co-researchers. For example, tapes can be
shown to (or in the case of audiotapes, played for) participants to get their interpretation of what was occurring and
how the taped events relate to sociohistorical features of the
culture, as illustrated in the following description.

EXAMPLE 1.15

VIEWING VIDEOTAPES WITH RESEARCH PARTICIPANTS
TO ENHANCE DATA ANALYSIS AND INTERPRETATION

Researchers Nastasi and her colleagues were conducting an ethnographic study of a
fifth-grade classroom. The classroom teacher (co-researcher, Braunhardt) requested
the opportunity to view videotapes with one of the other researchers (Nastasi) in an
effort to learn about the process of analyzing and interpreting observational data. As
they viewed the tapes, the researcher and teacher-researcher engaged in a dialogue
about the teacher's interpretation of what was happening as students worked together

on complex mathematical problem-solving tasks. During this discussion, the teacher shared valuable information about the students, her teaching philosophy and practices, and the culture of the school. For example, in one videotaped session, two students were engaged in ongoing conflict that interfered with the performance of the group (of four students) in which they were working. In the process of explaining how she intervened to end the conflict, the teacher-researcher indicated that one of these students was frequently engaged in similar conflicts in other settings within the school. Furthermore, she explained how the principal's expectations about discipline affected how she intervened. The joint viewing of the videotapes provided important insights from a key participant (teacher) and ultimately influenced both data analysis and interpretation (Nastasi et al., 1995; Nastasi & Young, 1994; Young et al., 1996).

Third, tapes provide a mechanism for promoting participants' self-reflection and learning. For example, tapes provide a permanent record that can be reviewed and discussed with participants to encourage self-evaluation and, if necessary, behavior change.

EXAMPLE 1.16

VIEWING VIDEOTAPES WITH RESEARCH PARTICIPANTS
TO ENCOURAGE SELF-REFLECTION AND BEHAVIOR CHANGE

In an ethnographic study of school-age children, videotaped episodes provided the basis for identifying and discussing the collaboration strategies that students had used in the classroom. The purpose of the discussions was to gather data about the students' experiences in cooperative learning activities. Dyads (pairs of students) who had worked together were asked to reflect on what had occurred during a recorded episode, using queries such as "Describe how you worked together," "What happened?" "How did you respond to your partner?" "How did you settle that disagreement?" The students were asked to discuss the perceived effectiveness of their collaboration techniques and to consider alternative approaches to collaboration; for example, "Did the way you settled that disagreement work for you?" "Were both partners contributing to the task?" "What else could each of you have done to encourage your partner to contribute ideas?" "How else could you have resolved the disagreement?" The discussions evolved into opportunities to promote reflection and learning. Subsequently, the ethnographer, the classroom teacher, and the students themselves reported related behavior changes (e.g., use of alternative techniques that had been generated during the discussions). Additionally, students reported increased monitoring of their collaborative interactions (Nastasi et al., 1995; Nastasi & Young, 1994; Young et al., 1996).

➤•➤•➤

Fourth, tapes provide a mechanism for disseminating findings. Tapes can be used for presentation of research findings, for training staff in future projects, and for demonstrating target intervention strategies or outcomes. If you intend to use tapes for demonstration and dissemination purposes, it is critical that taping quality is optimal and that you secure permission from participants for these purposes. In preparing tape segments for presentation purposes, it is preferable to develop separate tapes of the selected segments. Professional videotape equipment is available to assist you in this process.

Cross Reference: See Books 1 and 6 for discussions of informant permissions, privacy, and confidentiality

Using Audiovisual Technology to Foster Integration of Research and Practice

Audiovisual technology, particularly videotaping, can play an important role in promoting the integration of research and applied work (practice) in education, psychology, and anthropology. The examples presented in this chapter involved the use of audiovisual technology for the purposes of designing or studying interventions in applied (school and community) contexts. Some of the insights gained from this work suggest important future directions.

Using audiovisual technology to facilitate the development of culture-specific interventions. For example, joint viewing of videotapes of classroom instruction with teachers and/or students can be used to (a) gain insights about sociocultural influences on instructional practices, and (b) influence instructional practices. In an earlier example, joint viewing of videotapes with the classroom teacher led the teacher to reconsider how she handled student conflicts in her classroom (Young et al., 1996).

EXAMPLE 1.17

VIEWING VIDEOTAPES WITH RESEARCH PARTICIPANTS
TO DEVELOP CULTURE-SPECIFIC INTERVENTIONS

During the videotaped session, the teacher (Braunhardt) intervened and stopped the argument between two students, refocusing them on the assigned task. As the two students continued to interact during the remainder of the class session and into the next day's session, the ongoing conflict continued to erupt, particularly when the teacher was not present. The teacher (during viewing of the tapes) noted that her effort to stop the conflict had only a temporary impact, and that it may have been better to work with the students to help them negotiate their own resolution. The teacher, however, also noted that the expectation of the school's principal was to intervene immediately with any student conflicts in order to minimize the amount of time off-task. This teacher was so impressed by this experience that she noted in a presentation to the school board (conducted with researchers Young and Nastasi) that she had learned the importance of teaching students how to resolve their own conflicts.

Using audiovisual technology for staff development. As the preceding example suggests, videotapes of interventions (e.g., classroom instruction) can provide practitioners (e.g., teachers) with the opportunity to engage in reflection on their own practice, and subsequently influence future practices. This outcome was serendipitous. In other work cited in this chapter (Schensul et al., 1997), videotapes of intervention sessions were used for the specific purpose of staff development of the group facilitators who implemented the community-based intervention program for adolescent girls and their mothers, as described in Example 1.18.

EXAMPLE 1.18

VIEWING VIDEOTAPES WITH RESEARCH PARTICIPANTS FOR STAFF DEVELOPMENT

Archival data (videotaped sessions) from pilot intervention sessions provided the means for verifying accurate application of intervention techniques, tracking progress of group facilitators, and determining the need for additional staff training. Staff development consultants and group facilitators first reviewed tapes independently to examine and evaluate application of specified intervention techniques. Then, the consultants and facilitators together reviewed tape segments, discussed the accuracy and effectiveness of strategies, and identified objectives for subsequent training.

Using audiovisual technology to enhance intervention programs. Videotapes of individuals in natural contexts can be used as an intervention tool. That is, taped segments can be reviewed by interventionists (e.g., group facilitators) to (a) identify targets for change (e.g., communication patterns among group members), (b) monitor participants' reactions to specific intervention techniques (e.g., how group members respond to modeling of effective communication strategies), and (c) track the progress toward program goals (e.g., whether group members improve in their conflict resolution strategies over time). Furthermore, viewing tapes with target individuals (e.g., group members) can foster self-evaluation of their behavior or skills and facilitate subsequent development of plans for behavior change or skill development. Use of videotapes to foster self-modeling (i.e., by viewing oneself exhibiting exemplary behavior on edited videotapes) is an effective tool for promoting behavior change (Kehle & Gonzales, 1991).

Using audiovisual technology for program evaluation purposes. Taped segments provide archival data that can be reviewed repeatedly for different evaluation purposes. In the following example (Schensul et al., 1997), videotapes used for staff development purposes also provided a database for program evaluation.

EXAMPLE 1.19

USING ARCHIVAL VIDEOTAPED DATA FOR PROGRAM EVALUATION

The videotapes of intervention sessions provided the basis for evaluating the effectiveness of specific intervention strategies (e.g., modeling) in promoting target skill development (e.g., effective conflict resolution). Archival tapes could be randomly sampled, selecting a portion (e.g., 25%) of the sessions for transcribing and coding. The remaining (75%) tape sessions provided additional data, such as documentation of what occurred during the 25% of the sessions, or exploration of additional questions: What facilitator strategies were particularly effective in the girls-only compared to mother-only or mother-daughter groups? Was the content of the program curriculum appropriate for both adolescent girls and their mothers? Furthermore, tapes provided a record of the progress of program participants in developing target skills (e.g., communication and decision making).

Using audiovisual technology to facilitate communication with research participants. Audiotapes and videotapes can be used to gather additional data from research participants. For example, after listening to audiotaped segments from interviews, participants can be asked to elaborate further on their responses. Alternatively, videotaped observations could be used to gather interpretations from participants about their own behavior. Furthermore, taped segments could be used in dissemination efforts with participant groups to gain their input and garner support for intervention efforts.

With technological advances, the potential application and sophistication of audiovisual technology is unlimited. The capacity for interactive video, computer-video links, graphic displays, and computer voice recognition will likely influence the ways in which we are able to use audiovisual technology for ethnographic research. It is likely, for example, that voice recognition technology will permit direct transcription from audiotapes. The combination of interactive video, computer-video links, graphic representation, and voice recognition may make manual transcription unnecessary and permit us to view videotapes via computer and orally enter our codes and interpretations into the data set. These technological advances are likely to enhance the capacity for sharing data with participants and presenting findings to researchers and practitioners.

The capacity for personalized compact audiorecorders (e.g., individuals wearing individual microphones and recorders) already exists. This permits, for example, individuals to go about their routine activities and record all their verbal interactions with others as well as their personal reflections. Videocameras are becoming more compact; it is possible that we might one day equip participants with personal videocams for recording the events, sights, and sounds that they encounter. Such technological advances would revolutionize our notion of the key informant (i.e., a well-informed insider to the culture). However, the availability of these personalized recording devices also raises issues about informed consent of those individuals who are being recorded.

Cross Reference: See Books 1 and 6 for more information on researcher roles and collaboration among research team members

In spite of the potential technological advances, some issues are likely to remain unchanged. For example, the ethnographer's presence in the culture or context under study and direct interactions with participants are likely to continue to be critical to the research process. The conceptual issues, such as the role of theory, the researcher's focus, and the selection or development of a coding scheme, will remain important. The advantages of collaboration among researchers, coders, and participants are likely to remain critical for ensuring accuracy of data analysis and interpretation.

In conclusion, audiovisual technology is likely to become as common as fieldnotes in the tools of ethnography. The effective use of this technology requires that researchers and interventionists develop relevant technological expertise and continue to stay abreast of technological advances. At the same time, it is critical that ethnographers give serious consideration to the integration of this technology in ways that enhance research, theory development, and intervention.

NOTE

1. Although this section focuses specifically on using videotaped data, the same principles apply to audiotaped data.

REFERENCES

Bakeman, R., & Gottman, J. M. (1986). *Observing interaction: An introduction to sequential analysis.* New York: Cambridge University Press.

Clements, D. H., & Nastasi, B. K. (1988). Social and cognitive interactions in educational computer environments. *American Educational Research Journal, 25,* 87-106.

Kehle, T. J., & Gonzales, F. (1991). Self-modeling for children's emotional and social concerns. In P. W. Dowrick (Ed.), *Practical guide to using video in the behavioral sciences* (pp. 244-255). New York: John Wiley.

Nastasi, B. K., Bingham, A., & Clements, D. H. (1993, April). *Study of social processes in cooperative learning environments: The qualitative-quantitative mix.* Paper presented at the annual meeting of the American Educational Research Association, Atlanta, GA.

Nastasi, B. K., & Clements, D. H. (1992). Social-cognitive behaviors and higher-order thinking in educational computer environments. *Learning and Instruction, 2,* 215-238.

Nastasi, B. K., & Clements, D. H. (1994). *Observational coding scheme for interactive social-cognitive behaviors.* Unpublished manuscript, State University of New York at Albany.

Nastasi, B. K., Clements, D. H., & Battista, M. T. (1990). Social-cognitive interactions, motivation, and cognitive growth in Logo programming and CAI problem-solving environments. *Journal of Educational Psychology, 82,* 150-158.

Nastasi, B. K., Johnson, J., & Owens, B. (1995, April). *Ethnographic study of collaborative problem solving in a fifth-grade interactive video context.*

Paper presented at the annual meeting of the American Educational Research Association, San Francisco.

Nastasi, B. K., Schensul, J. J., deSilva, M. W. A., Varjas, K., Silva, K. T., Ratnayake, P., & Schensul, S. L. (in press). Community-based sexual risk prevention program for Sri Lankan youth: Influencing sexual-risk decision making. *International Quarterly of Community Health Education, 18*(1).

Nastasi, B. K., Varjas, K., Sarkar, S., & Jayasena, A. (1998). Participatory model of mental health programming: Lessons learned from work in a developing country. *School Psychology Review, 27*(2), 260-276.

Nastasi, B. K., & Young, M. (1994, June-July). *Ethnographic study of collaborative and mathematical problem solving.* Paper presented at the sixth annual convention of the American Psychological Society, Washington, DC.

Schensul, J., Berg, M., & Romero, M. (1997). *Using process evaluation to improve staff facilitation skills in a group-norms based intervention with female adolescents.* Paper presented at annual evaluation meeting of the Center for Substance Abuse Prevention, Washington, DC.

Silva, K. T., Ratnayake, P., Schensul, S., Schensul, J., deSilva, M. W., Nastasi, B., Wedisinghe, P. K., Sivayoganathan, C., Aponso, H., Eisenberg, M., & Lewis, J. (1997). *Youth and sexual risk in Sri Lanka.* Washington, DC: International Center for Research on Women.

VideoToolkit™ *user's guide.* (1992). Millis, MA: Abbate Video.

Young, M. F., Nastasi, B. K., & Braunhardt, L. (1996). Implementing Jasper Immersion: A case of conceptual change. In B. Wilson (Ed.), *Constructivist learning environments: Case studies in instructional design* (pp. 121-134). Englewood Cliffs, NJ: Educational Technology Publications.

SUGGESTED RESOURCES

VideoToolkit™ *user's guide.* (1992). Millis, MA: Abbate Video.

Video Toolkit™ (1992) is a videotape logging and editing package made for use with Macintosh computers. The software makes it possible to perform videotape logging and editing functions from your computer, thus facilitating the coordination of transcription and tape logging/editing. Using the computer and one (source) video device, you are able to control video search and playback options via the computer. With a second (recording) video device, you are able to control the logging and assembly of video segments. This software is particularly useful for managing a video database and developing video presentations. The software is available from Abbate Video, Inc., 14 Ross Avenue, Floor 3, Millis, MA 02054.

Bakeman, R., & Gottman, J. M. (1986). *Observing interaction: An introduction to sequential analysis.* New York: Cambridge University Press.

This book is an excellent resource for conducting observations of ongoing social interactions and analyzing the sequential nature of such interactions. The authors provide valuable information on the conduct of systematic observations, development of coding schemes, establishing interrater agreement, and sequential analysis of interactions. The text is particularly useful for those interested in the quantitative analysis of videotaped data.

Miles, M. B., & Huberman, A. M. (1994). *Qualitative analysis: An expanded sourcebook* (2nd ed.). Thousand Oaks, CA: Sage.

This book is an excellent resource for conducting qualitative analysis of both audiotaped and videotaped data. The authors provide valuable information on the coding and display of such data.

2

FOCUSED GROUP INTERVIEWS

Jean J. Schensul

INTRODUCTION

This chapter will provide readers with guided instruction in conducting focused group interviews. We choose to use the term "focused group interview," rather than the more frequently used "focus group," because the focus group is only one form of group interview. We begin by defining what a group interview is.

WHAT IS A GROUP INTERVIEW?

A group interview is any discussion held between a researcher and more than one other individual. Group interviews can be used for many purposes: to collect information on a cultural domain, to develop listings for pilesorts, to identify the range of variation in opinions or attitudes on a set of topics, to collect simple numerical data on reported experiences, or to react to the results of previously collected data (Scrimshaw, 1992). Group interviews may be formal or informal, preorganized or occurring in natural settings, guided to a greater or lesser degree by the anthropologist/ facilitator, and more or less open-ended. Group interviews are interactive; members are encouraged to express their opinions and to dialogue about them with one another.

Group interviews are useful for

- Orienting oneself to a new field of study
- Generating hypotheses based on informants' insights
- Evaluating different research sites or study populations
- Developing individual questions for interview schedules and questionnaires
- Obtaining participants' interpretations of results gathered in earlier research studies (Morgan, 1988; Stewart & Shamdasani, 1990).

Group interviews have a number of advantages.

Group interviews

- Generate a considerable quantity of data in a relatively short period from a larger number of people than would be possible by interviewing key informants only.
- Allow the researcher to record and analyze group members' reactions to ideas and to each other.
- Produce data and insights that would be less accessible without the interaction found in a group (Morgan, 1988, p. 12).
- Elicit useful "natural language discourse" that allows the researcher to learn idiomatic expressions, common terminology, and communication patterns in the community in a rapid and concise manner.

As a researcher, you might decide to conduct a series of group interviews under the following circumstances.

You need to gain a lot of information in a short period of time. Group interviews are efficient. Individual interviews offer opportunities to collect a great deal of data on a single respondent's perceptions, values, vocabulary, and personal experiences, but they can take a long time. To assess how this information fits with other individuals' experiences in the same community, up to 30 additional individual interviews could be necessary. Even interviews that cover fewer topics can take up to 1 hour.

The group interview, on the other hand, elicits extensive information from a more broadly representative number of people in a relatively shorter period of time. The average group interview takes from 45 minutes to no more than $1\frac{1}{2}$ hours and includes at least five individuals. Because it can take twice as long to write up the results of an interview (or to transcribe tapes) as the interview itself, the group interview is far more efficient, at least from the point of view of the interviewer.

You encounter an opportunity to conduct an informal group interview in the field. Field situations provide many occasions where people gather casually, and opportunities to discuss topics of mutual interest arise. In rural areas of Sri Lanka, women gather several times a day to bathe or to wash clothing on the rocks by the side of a river. In Lima, Peru, family members gather around a common water tap. In Kenya, Masai women walk together for 4 or 5 miles each morning and evening to obtain much needed water. In parts of the American South, people may gather to assist in the construction of a house. In small-town Mexico in 1970, teachers gathered after school every Friday to drink cola and brandy and discuss the affairs of the week. In Hartford, Connecticut, girls 9 to 12 years of age travel home two nights per week in a program van. In Chicago, office staff in a school change program meet once a week for administrative purposes and generally spend 15 minutes waiting for all of the members of the group to gather, during which time they chat about topics of common interest. It is always tempting for the researcher in the field to see these "interludes" or "transitions" as opportunities to relax, to allow the mind to wander, and to let the guard down. Instead, they should be seen as opportunities to gather information from small groups that could not be obtained in any other way.

You want to observe how people interact with one another around an issue. In field settings, participant observers or other observers may be able to observe members of the community or institution engaged in discussions and debate or differences of opinion with one another. Observation of such debates is quite informative. The debates reveal both differences of position and perspective in a group and ways in which that group deals with conflict. However, such debates or discussions do not occur very often, and if they do, the researcher may not observe them. Or, the topics chosen for debate by ordinary people in the course of ordinary discussion are not those in which the researcher is interested. Under such circumstances, you could organize a more formal focus group, where the researcher can present problems of interest in a structured environment so that participants consider these problems rather than those they might select themselves.

You want to obtain ethnographic data through group instruction. Instructors or group leaders in educational programs, or health or other kinds of interventions, can use group discussions as an opportunity to learn about the ways in which participants are thinking and making decisions about a topic. In such situations, the instructor/facilitator can pose a problem or dilemma of some sort. For example, a class in social problem solving might be asked to discuss in small or large groups what to do about a problem in which a middle school female student is harassed by male students on the way home from school every day. The ensuing discussion can reveal much about the differing beliefs held by participants, whether or not they have enough information to understand or address the problem, what actions they might take to solve it, and what differences in option or action exist among them. This is useful information for monitoring the problem-solving progress of the group during the instruction period. It can also be used in evaluating the longer term success of the instructional effort.

You want an efficient way to construct locally valid or meaningful surveys. Quantifiable survey data are usually collected with instruments in which the responses to questions are predetermined and limited in number. Researchers face two major challenges in the creation of valid and reliable questionnaires, especially in new and culturally different field situations. These challenges are

— to identify the appropriate questions, and
— to identify the appropriate response alternatives.

It is always better if researchers have a relatively long period of time in which to engage in initial ethnography—talking to key informants, conducting in-depth interviews, engaging in participant observation, and mapping the community. However, when time and other resources are short and researchers do not know whether they have captured all of the questions or discovered every important alternative response, focused group interviews can be extremely useful.

You want to field test a survey or other quantitative instrument for coherence. You may have developed your own survey based on ethnographic field research, or you may have chosen to use an already existing instrument, scale, or other measure in a new field setting. Even instruments based on ethnographic field research should be discussed with local experts to clarify correct use of language, address translation issues, and ensure comprehension. These discussions and reviews become especially important when instruments to be used in your field situation have been developed elsewhere. The concepts, language, and mode of expression all need to be validated in the local context. One good way to test such instruments is to use focus groups to determine whether people understand the questions (Krueger, 1988).

INFORMAL VERSUS FORMAL GROUP INTERVIEWS

Group interviews range along a continuum of specificity, from informal to formal. This continuum is summarized in the following table.

Highly Informal	*Highly Formal*
Timing spontaneous and not previously determined	Timing carefully preplanned and prescheduled
Interview takes place in naturalistic setting chosen by participants	Interview takes place in planned or contrived setting chosen by the interviewer
Interview is interactive and takes place in the normal course of conversation or activity	Interview is directed in the form of questions that call for response; no interactive discussion between facilitator and respondents, although interaction may be encouraged among respondents
Size of the group subject to natural conditions in the field and not controlled by the field researcher	Size is strictly controlled in advance, and only those invited are admitted to the interview
Respondents are self-selected	Respondents are preselected
Never an incentive	Always an incentive
Few predetermined questions; interview subject to interviewing skills and knowledge of the field researcher at the moment	All questions are predetermined, although probes may be used by the interviewer
Researcher has an already established relationship with the group	Researcher may have no relationship with the group, although the best interviews are conducted by those with extensive prior knowledge of the subject

It is important to keep in mind that the group interview is one among a series of interactive approaches to the collection of qualitative and quantitative ethnographic data and should never be considered as a replacement for other forms of data collection. Furthermore, the results of the interview are best understood and interpreted in the context of other data on the community or situation in question.

Informal Group Interviewing

The informal group interview has a long history in qualitative/ethnographic research. Most field researchers who gather information in naturalistic settings find themselves at one time or another talking informally with a group about one or more topics of mutual interest. These discussions can occur in the most informal settings, or they can occur in more formalized settings that begin as an individual interview and expand.

EXAMPLE 2.1

FROM INFORMAL TO FORMAL GROUP INTERVIEWS: SRI LANKA

A group of American social scientists that included Stephen and Jean Schensul visited a clinic in Kandy, Sri Lanka, in which they were expecting to watch a team of Western and Ayurveda-trained physicians administer a combination of Ayurvedic decoctions to juvenile diabetics that was designed to reduce their dependence on injected insulin. As they were observing and learning about the record-keeping system that patients were requested to keep for physicians, a second Ayurvedic physician joined the conversation, followed by a clinic nurse and two more patients. Suddenly, what was intended to be a straightforward demonstration followed by discussion with the two physicians turned into a group discussion of Ayurveda versus Western medicine, ways of working together, ways of preparing and storing decoctions, and so on.

In this instance, the social scientists drew upon their knowledge of similar circumstances as well as their own intuitive curiosity to maximize the opportunities for discussion and debate. Each group member—there were four social scientists, three medical anthropologists, and a sociologist—had his or her own series of questions that had to be negotiated in the context of this informal group interview.

EXAMPLE 2.2

NEGOTIATING QUESTION SEQUENCES IN
AN INFORMAL GROUP INTERVIEW: CHINA

On another occasion, Jean Schensul accompanied Chinese colleagues on a field visit to a village doctor and pharmacy in a rural area of Hunan to determine the degree to which materials and information on the prevention of pneumonia had penetrated the everyday practice of physicians. The project principal investigator (PI), a Chinese physician familiar with both Chinese and Western medicine and from that geographic area, conducted the interview. Within 15 minutes, the pharmacy was surrounded by several hundred people. They, in turn, invited several other village physicians to participate in the interview. The PI took advantage of the opportunity to question the other village physicians and discovered that their approaches to instruction and early symptom identification, as well as their use of nationally distributed health education materials, were quite different and not necessarily consistent with the nationally promoted intervention program.

Most field research experiences are filled with similar opportunities in which people gather informally around an event often stimulated by the presence of the researcher. In such situations, researchers can take advantage of the moment by asking the key members of the group a series of questions designed to

- Explore a theme
- Identify differences of opinion or action across individuals (i.e., capture the range of variation in the group)

- Define terminology
- Obtain a history of a situation or event

When more than one field researcher is involved in the informal interview, as in the case of the first vignette, interviewers must be aware of one another's interests and perspectives and leave time for others to ask questions. Interviewers must always be conscious of the potential status and gender differences in the overall group and make sure that each interviewer has an opportunity to ask questions.

The best way to prepare for informal group interviews is to maintain constant vigilance in relation to the data you are collecting in the field and to carry a small notebook or electronic device in which you can list new ideas, questions, hunches, and concepts. Vigilance during participant observation is the best way to "find" informal individual and group interviews. If researchers are continuously aware of the purpose of their research; what kinds of information are missing or need to be expanded upon; and which hunches, hypotheses, or conceptual models are emerging from field data that need to be tested or confirmed, then informal interviews can be valuable adjuncts to more formalized data collection. However, because informal opportunities to talk with groups of people occur in unpredictable ways and at unpredictable times, it is often said that ethnographers never leave the field.

Formal Focused Group Interviews

At the more organized end of the group interview continuum is the formal focused group interview. Such an interview involves from 5 to 15 individuals[1] from representative groups of people. Under the direction of a group leader or facilitator, these individuals are asked to respond to a previously determined set of questions on a specific topic over a period of not more than about 90 minutes. Participants may receive an incentive (either money or a gift with financial worth) to compensate them for time and information.

EXAMPLE 2.3

FORMAL FOCUS GROUP WITH OLDER ADULTS ADDICTED TO INJECTION DRUGS

A group of five older drug addicts was invited to a special meeting at the Institute for Community Research to discuss the group members' history of drug use, ways in which drug users over 50 years of age obtain and use drugs, and their relationships with younger drug users. The older addicts were identified by a member of the research team. A considerable amount of information was already available about both the target population and the individuals identified to take part in the focus group discussion. They were personally acquainted with the research team through other interviews and interventions; furthermore, they were known to have expertise in the three areas to be addressed in the interview. Based on prior experience, the research team knew that this group of five was well informed, would feel comfortable in a group interview, and would be able to provide valuable information (Kim Radda, personal communication, 1998).

◆•◆•◆

The formal focus group technique appeared in the 1930s as an alternative to direct interviews at a point where quantitative researchers were exploring alternatives to survey research. During the 1940s, at the onset of World War II, prominent American anthropologists such as Mead and Benedict used direct and indirect qualitative research methods to study national character. At the same time, sociologists such as Lazarsfeld and Merton explored the use of focus groups for assessing media effects on attitudes toward America's involvement in the war (Stewart & Shamdasani, 1990). Working for the Columbia University Office of Radio Research, they recruited groups of people to respond to radio programs designed to boost morale with regard to the war effort. Listeners were asked to press buttons depending on whether their reaction to the radio message was positive or negative. Subsequently, they were asked about their reasons for reacting as they did (Merton, 1987). The two critical elements in this experiment, which continue to constitute important aspects of formal group interviewing, are recording people's responses at the moment or in face-to-face interaction, and administering strategically targeted or "focused" interviews designed to obtain information on themes deemed important by the investigators.

These techniques have been used in advertising from the mid-1940s on, but it was not until the 1970s that, along with other qualitative data collection techniques, the "focus group" came to be seen as a legitimate means of collecting information in field settings in the social sciences. Nowadays, some researchers view focus groups as a replacement for survey research because they are perceived to be less expensive than surveys while providing more information than individual interviews about how people think and feel about products or issues. More recently, focus groups are being used to study knowledge, attitudes, and beliefs in a variety of social situations and have become a widely accepted means of collecting formative, process, and outcome data in programs addressing a variety of means of introducing, stimulating, or supporting social change. Indeed, some methodologists have said that formal focus groups are the only way of collecting qualitative data. We do not agree that focus groups are a substitute for surveys, nor do we think that they are the "only way to collect qualitative data." However, we do believe that group interviews can provide large amounts of data in relatively short periods of time, provided that they are set in the context of other data collection efforts and that the data collected are appropriate to the focus group format. Furthermore, before focus groups are used, careful thought must be given to why data should be collected in a group format; what kinds of data are needed; and under what circumstances, by whom, and how the data will be used.

ORGANIZING AND PREPARING FOR FOCUSED GROUP INTERVIEWS

Ethnographers cannot always just "wait around" for group discussions to happen. Sometimes, the ethnographer must create the opportunity for discussion. Formal focus group sessions call for careful consideration of

- The topic of the interviews
- Characteristics of the target populations
- Creation of comparison groups
- How to set up the interview
- Conduct of the interview once it is organized

Determining the Focus of the Formal Group Interview

The first step in preparing for a more formal interview is to determine the focus of the interview. It is important to keep in mind that the average group meeting is approximately 90 to 120 minutes long, and that up to 30% of this time is devoted to organizing and informal socializing. Thus, the range and scope of the topics addressed in a single focus group session are somewhat limited. On one hand, focus group discussions offer the opportunity for flexibility in question and response, and they may generate new ideas and information. On the other hand, respondents can become easily bored with a discussion if it is *too* focused. The success of focus groups depends a great deal on balancing breadth and depth of participation within a restricted time period.

We suggest that formal focus group discussions should center on the relationship between **target populations** and

Definition: Target population is the people the researcher wants to study or to affect

a single **cultural domain**. Among cultural domains often addressed by social scientists are "sports," "drug use," "dietary patterns," "contraceptive choices," "street life," "health practices," "religious beliefs and preferences," or "secular institutional affiliations" (Spradley, 1979; Trotter & Schensul, 1998). Each of these domains is broad enough so that both facilitators and participants can identify and discuss a variety of subdomains or subtopics. A prepared facilitator will have considered the most important subtopics for discussion well in advance of the session and will be prepared to identify and ask questions about subdomains that are not identified by participants in the course of the focus group discussion.

Definition: Cultural domains are the major category of beliefs, attitudes, behaviors, perceptions, or policies that constitutes the focus of the study

Cross Reference: See Book 3, Chapter 3, for more information on researching cultural domains

Deciding Upon the Target Population and Recruiting the Sample

Choosing a Target Population

Three important factors influence choice of the target population:

1. The purpose of the study
2. Whom the study is intended to help
3. For whom the information generated from the study is intended

It would not make sense to conduct focus groups with non-Puerto Rican women in a study of how best to reach middle-aged Puerto Rican women at risk for Type II or adult onset diabetes. As in the example below, it might also be important to consider whether to include middle-aged men or young women, and Spanish-only versus bilingual or English-speaking women in the study population.

EXAMPLE 2.4

DECIDING ON FOCUS GROUP REPRESENTATION:
TYPE II DIABETES IN PUERTO RICAN ADULTS

A team of anthropologists, mass media experts, and community leaders were developing a project designed to reach Puerto Rican women between the ages of 45 and 60 who were potentially at high risk for onset of insulin-dependent Type II diabetes. To assist in the formation of a mass media campaign, as well as strategies for direct communication regarding the need for screening, symptom reporting, and regular clinic visits, focus groups were planned with the target population (i.e., Spanish-speaking women of the target age group). The team spent several planning sessions collecting information to help them decide whether it was worthwhile to interview several other groups, including men who were partners and caregivers of female diabetics, younger women caregivers, and English-speaking Puerto Rican women. Considering time, money, and cultural factors, the team decided to conduct formative focus groups with women at the upper and lower end of the at-risk age continuum. Because men were not seen as sources of support and information to the women, they were not included in the formative Formal Focus Group Sample. However, men *were* included in the evaluation, because both components of the campaign were intended to have secondary influence on male partners' knowledge and behavior (Henrietta Bernal, personal communication, 1998).

Generally a focus group study will include at least two, and more often three or four, different classes or types of people to ensure representativeness—for example, adult males and females 18 to 39 years of age, and those 40 and older; first-generation adolescents representing African, Puerto Rican, Mexican, Native American, Cambodian, Irish, Russian, Polish, and Italian ethnic groups; urban, suburban, and rural residents, and so on.

EXAMPLE 2.5

COMPARING AND TRIANGULATING DATA
ON PUERTO RICAN CHILDREN'S ACTIVITIES
ACROSS THREE DIFFERENT GROUPS

A study of Puerto Rican children's energy expenditures called for creating a list of activities in which children between the ages of 7 and 10 typically engage. To obtain this list, with an explanation of the meaning of the activities, researchers Schensul and Diaz held focus group discussions with the children in two mixed first- and second-grade bilingual classes. They then interviewed a group of 10 mothers, as well as teachers and after-school program workers, to obtain and verify a complete list of Puerto Rican children's activities and to obtain information about where, at what time of day, during what season of the year, and how often each day or week these activities took place (Schensul, Diaz, & Woolley, 1996).

Creating a Representative
Sample for a Focus Group

Focused group interviewing uses a **quota sampling** procedure. Quota sampling assumes diversity within a target population. The first step in quota sampling is to identify major sources of diversity or variation in the community of interest that are believed to be significant to the study. Focus groups are then organized to include representation from these sectors. Depending on the purpose of the study, focus groups may include representatives of all sectors, or separate focus groups may be held for each one of the major sectors in the target population. If group interviews occur in natural settings, the researcher should know the distribution of status, power, and interests in the broader community and how to put in context the perspectives of group members who represent various interests and constituen-

Definition: Quota sampling involves selecting equal numbers of respondents to represent each characteristic, group, or sector within a population

cies. Considerable thought must be given to the representativeness of group membership and to the combination of individuals that is most likely to produce rich data. Organizing homogeneous focus groups—by gender, age, ethnicity, education level, and so on—should be considered when heterogeneity could hamper discussion. For example, gender-mixed groups may not feel comfortable at first discussing topics related to sex, power, or abuse. Heterogeneous groupings are useful if the ethnographer knows that diversity will produce lively interaction.

> *Methods for Creating*
> *a Quota Sampling Frame*[2]
>
> ■ Generate a model of groups suspected to exist in the target population.
> ■ Use previously generated data to identify groups in the target population.
> ■ Conduct a study to create your own profile of characteristics in the target population.

There are several ways to determine adequate representation. The first method requires the ethnographer to generate a hypothetical predictive model. Based on prior firsthand knowledge of the community (from literature, key informants, and personal experience), the ethnographer creates a set of hunches about what the major grouping categories are in the target population. The second method is to use previous research or other accessible sources of secondary data on the community or target population. The third method involves creating a profile of community characteristics by questioning natural groups in the community that are known to differ in many ways, until the "saturation point" is reached, that is, until no new responses are obtained. It is important to hold some important char-

acteristics constant—such as ethnicity, ability level, gender—in each focus group. This means that all members of
a given group will be identical on that particular characteristic, although they may vary considerably on other characteristics. It is equally important to include representatives
from a sufficient number of groups to capture the potential range of variation in the overall target population—
including ethnic variation, gender differences, age groupings, place of residence, type of work, and so on.

A number of researchers suggest that ethnographers
must conduct at least two focus groups for each variable of
concern to ensure that they capture most aspects related to
the subject of inquiry (Khan, Patel, & Hemlatha, 1990). For
example, if two variables are considered, such as age and
work patterns, at least four focus groups should be held: a
minimum of two groups representing participants from
two different "age groupings" (perhaps older and younger,
or under/over 35 years of age); and two more groups representing two different categories of "work patterns."

Age	Work Type	
	Vendors/Hawkers	Service/Sector
35 and Over	1	1
Under 35	1	1

Of course, researchers could hold one focus group with
representatives from each group, or they could conduct
more focus groups for each variable if there are reasons to
subdivide the variables further (e.g., into three or more
appropriate age groupings, or categories of work).

If four variables, such as age, sex, caste, and use of illicit substances, are considered, a minimum of eight categories would be required, two for each variable. These categories could be the basis of individual focused group interviews, or representatives from each category could be included in one heterogeneous focus group. However, age, caste or class, and use of illicit substances are all possibly more complicated than they appear. In a drug study being conducted in Hartford, Connecticut, for example, three age categories—18 to 24, 25 to 39, and 40 and over—emerged as important. In addition, three categories of drug users have emerged from ethnographic and quantitative data: those using "gateway drugs" (marijuana, alcohol, and cigarettes); those snorting or sniffing cocaine and/or heroin; and those using drugs intravenously. Three class categories are also important: urban unemployed, urban employed, and suburban employed people. The number of separate focus groups necessary to capture variation by age, gender, drug use, and class in this instance is 54, obtained by multiplying Gender × Age × Class × Type of Drug Use.

Gender   =   2 × (male, female)

Age   =   3 × (18 to 24, 25 to 39, 40 and over)

Class   =   3 × (urban unemployed, urban employed, suburban employed)

Drug use   =   3 (gateway, cocaine/heroin, intravenous)

Total number of categories or groups (2 × 3 × 3 × 3) = 54

The total number of groups required for this study is 54. Obviously, because staff, time, and financial resources are limited, researchers will need to determine which differences are most important in accurately representing the target community. Decisions about the appropriate number of focus groups can then be made accordingly.

EXAMPLE 2.6

DECIDING WHOM TO INTERVIEW AND HOW TO
RECRUIT RESPONDENTS IN AN HIV-RELATED STUDY

The Boulder County AIDS Project (BCAP) wanted to determine if the information campaign they had organized for HIV/AIDS prevention was reaching the rapidly growing population of Latino immigrants from the county. They hired Elias Martinez, a bilingual researcher from the University of Colorado, who grew up along the Texas/Mexico border, to conduct focus groups among groups in the Latino population. BCAP wanted to assess (a) levels of information—and disinformation—about HIV/AIDS and its transmission, (b) which sources of information Latinos in Boulder County used to find out about health care resources, (c) the extent to which Latinos used condoms and other means to prevent infection with HIV/AIDS, and (d) whether or not Latinos had seen or used the brochures and other materials on HIV/AIDS that BCAP had developed for use by health care workers in the county.

Knowing the population well, Martinez decided to select the following groups: one of adult males and one of adult female migrant workers; one including male and female Latino adolescents; one of male and one of female native-born U.S. citizens of Latino origin; one of male Latinos working as professionals or volunteers to improve the conditions of Latinos in Boulder County; and one of parents of elementary and middle school Latino children. The group of professionals was recruited through a network of like-minded colleagues. However, Martinez faced a number of difficulties in organizing the remaining five groups. First, many members of the migrant worker group were undocumented immigrants who feared being deported and were reluctant to talk with strangers. Martinez worked through an alcohol treatment center and a local clinic serving Latinos to find participants for the migrant worker and Chicano groups. Second, Martinez needed to secure parental permission before youths under the age of 18 could participate in the research. Contacting youth through the schools required equally time-consuming permissions from school district Institutional Review Boards. To resolve the problem, Martinez solicited participants from a youth group run by the local church diocese. Third, women, particularly the migrant workers, were reluctant to talk about sexual practices of any kind, especially to a male interviewer. Martinez hired a young Latina social worker to conduct these interviews by herself; she assisted him with the other interviews. Finally, many male members of the target population were reluctant to discuss a disease that they felt only homosexuals—which they denied being—could contract.

Martinez's knowledge of Latino cultural beliefs about sexual practices and homo-sexuality in general helped him tease out sources of bias and denial in these interviews (Martinez, 1996).

> Can the results of focus group interviews be generalized, or taken as representative of the larger population from which the focus group participants were drawn? If sampling methods are carefully spelled out, and if efforts to achieve representativeness are based on prior knowledge of the target populations, the results obtained through focused group interviews can be generalized with caution. Generalizability is especially warranted when responses create regular patterns. For example, if the researcher conducts five focused group interviews each with older and younger Chinese women living in Flushing, New York and finds that the within-age-group perspectives are consistently similar, and between-age-group perspectives are consistently different, he or she can feel more confident that the focus group responses reflect patterns prevailing in the larger population.

EXAMPLE 2.7 ➖•➖•➖

ENSURING GENERALIZABILITY IN FOCUSED GROUP INTERVIEWING: CONDUCTING FOCUS GROUPS WITH MEN AND WOMEN IN TWO GEOGRAPHICALLY DIFFERENT AREAS

In a city in the central highland area of Sri Lanka, two groups of male and female university students discussed how they believe HIV/AIDS to be contracted. They listed 12 ways, including sitting on a toilet seat used by a person with AIDS, mosquito bites, giving blood, touching the face of a person with HIV, and intimate sexual contact. When comparable focus groups were held in a low-income neighborhood near downtown, a shorter list that did not add any new items emerged. A scale of "ways of contracting AIDS" was developed that included all of the items. When this scale was reviewed with two additional groups, one in the community and one in the university, no new items emerged. Researchers could thus conclude that the listing was representative of the overall population of youth in the target population (Silva et al., 1997).

Summary. The purpose of focus group research is to identify important issues, domains for further investigation,
meanings, values, opinions, behaviors, and explanations for
cultural or physical phenomena. Focused group interviews
should identify important variations in these areas. But they
are not intended to identify the distribution of these opinions, meanings, issues, or behaviors in the target population. Quantitative survey research using random sampling
techniques is required for this purpose. Thus, it is important to keep in mind that random sampling is not important
and is probably not possible when selecting respondents for
group interviews.

Identifying and Recruiting Participants

Once a list of sampling categories has been identified,
ethnographers must identify and recruit participants. Some
of the main ways to identify participants are described
below.

■ *Creating a list.* The ethnographer creates a list of all people in
the desired category, based on knowledge he or she has about
people in the category. If the group generated by the list is
small—7 to 15 members—everyone on the list is invited to
participate, regardless of whether they know each other or not.
For example, a formative study to identify Puerto Rican families' perceptions of Alzheimer's disease (Schensul, Torres, &
Wetle, 1994) required a comparison of health care providers'
views of cognitive impairment with those of the families caring
for Alzheimer's victims. Only a small number of geriatricians
and social workers had experience with dementias—including
Alzheimer's disease. Because only 16 providers had such experience, all of them were invited to attend a focus group in
which symptoms of Alzheimer's disease were defined and
prioritized.

■ *Using a pre-existing telephone or mailing list.* It is always easier
to identify focus group members from a preexisting list. Lists
of individuals can sometimes be obtained from agencies, organizations, clubs, and membership groups when confidenti-

ality is not an issue. However, these lists may not identify individuals with the specific characteristics sought for your group. Thus, you will need to develop a screening tool that allows you to identify the appropriate candidates by age, gender, ethnicity, residence, specific behaviors, and so on.

■ *Advertising.* Clinical researchers often advertise in regional or local newspapers for subjects wishing to participate in clinical trials. For example, marijuana researchers at the University of Connecticut Health Center recruit through newspaper advertisements regular marijuana users who wish to quit, and osteoporosis researchers at a local health research center who are conducting clinical trials of new drugs advertise for women who are short, slim, postmenopausal, and not taking hormone replacements.

Cross Reference: For more information on different approaches to ethnographic sampling, see Book 1, Book 2, Chapter 9, and Book 4, Chapters 1 and 3

■ *Snowball or network sampling.* Snowball or network sampling techniques recruit initial or index individuals who then identify other people they know who possess the characteristics desired by the researcher (Trotter & Schensul, 1998; Watters & Biernacki, 1989). Network sampling begins by inviting a group of people who have either participated in a focus group or are appropriate candidates to bring or recommend for participation their friends or others they know who are like themselves. This strategy guarantees that at least some, but certainly not all, participants will know one another well.

■ *Asking for assistance from service organizations.* Ethnographers can identify service organizations that provide services to those people whom you would like to include in your focus groups. This strategy was used by Martinez in his work on the Boulder HIV/AIDS study. Such a strategy involves first contacting the director and other staff members who have access to such individuals. You will need to inform them in person about the nature of the research and the type of person you wish to recruit. Next, if they agree to help, you will need to provide them with information about the project, who is eligible to participate, how long it will take, and what participants will receive in the form of incentives.

■ *Enumerating.* In small community, neighborhood, or village settings, researchers can use an outreach and enumeration process involving door-to-door screening to identify candidates for focus group participation, and then invite those identified to attend focus groups. This process is more expensive than the others mentioned previously, but it is an excellent way of simultaneously identifying households both for focus group participation and selection for randomized survey sampling.

Once you have decided how to identify potential participants, you must contact them and invite them to participate in focus group sessions. Telephone invitations, followed by letters describing the purpose, content, structure, location, and sponsors of the focus groups, are important ways to legitimize the focus group sessions for prospective participants. It is always more effective if someone known to the respondents sends the invitation. In some instances, a home visit to potential participants is helpful in convincing them that the experience will be enjoyable for them. Focus group members may have transportation or baby-sitting needs, which should be identified beforehand. If incentives are used, they should be prepared in advance and be ready to give to participants immediately after the focus group session. Incentives are usually valued at between $10 and $25 and may consist of small amounts of cash, gift certificates, food vouchers, or other items considered appropriate in the setting. Focus group participants should be asked to sign vouchers when they receive their incentives, as a record of receipt.

Choosing an Appropriate Site for Focus Group Sessions

One of the most important considerations in ensuring focus group attendance is location. The four most important factors that define a good site for focus group discussions are

1. Comfort
2. Convenience
3. Potential for interruption
4. Noise level

Informal group interviews are held, of course, wherever people gather. If a group gathers long enough to be able to engage in a discussion (with or without the researcher), the location is sufficiently comfortable and convenient at least for the participants. Such locations include parks, street corners, marketplaces, water taps, river banks, bars, senior citizen centers, teachers' lounges, bowling alleys, and playgrounds.

Such informal locations are not always the best places for more formal focus groups. Formal focus groups require quiet; it is best to hold them in less public meeting places, such as small conference rooms in business or consulting settings; meeting spaces in churches; community-based organizations and other community locations; rooms in schools, universities, hospitals, and other institutions; or people's homes.

Site Selection Criteria for
Formal Group Interview Sessions

- Convenience
- Perceptions, or how participants feel about the site
- Accessibility
- Size
- Facilities and amenities

Convenience. Researchers need to know how convenient it is for participants to get to the location. Long distances, the high cost of transportation, difficulty in locating parking, the high cost of parking, or perceptions of safety in the neighborhood may be barriers to participation.

Perceptions. Researchers also must consider how participants feel about the location. Is it one normally used by the people who are to be invited? Do they see it as a place where they will feel welcome and comfortable, or will they feel like outsiders? We are not suggesting that focus groups always must be held in places used by participants. New places are quite appropriate and may even be of great interest to participants, as long as the places selected are not perceived as locations where they have been excluded in the past.

Accessibility. Another consideration is whether it is easy for participants to locate the meeting space in the building where the focus group is to be held. A hospital in Hartford is very generous with meeting space, but, with new construction and several new wings, the correct entrances are complicated to navigate. Once inside, the locations designated for public meetings are very difficult to find. One participant, searching for a focus group on child care, found herself at a reception with people who seemed friendly, and where food and coffee was being served. She stayed for almost an hour, waiting for the group to begin, before she discovered that the hospital information desk directed her to go to the wrong place. She missed the focus group session altogether (although she met a lot of very pleasant people!).

Size. A crucial consideration is size. Is there sufficient space to accommodate the size of the group? The space designated for the interview should be big enough, but also appropriate to group size. A small group, for example, will feel more comfortable if it meets in a smaller space rather than an auditorium.

Facilities and amenities. An important issue also is whether the location has the proper facilities and environment for conducting a more formal focused group interview. There should be enough comfortable chairs to accommodate everyone. Although it may be desirable to offer participants a writing surface, some focus group members may not wish to write or may not be able to write. Tables create social distance, and furniture should be flexible and easily movable so that decisions to keep or remove tables, couches, and so on can be made at the last minute. There should be a place for serving food and drinks, a blackboard or its equivalent, and sufficient light. Ideal circumstances for formal focus group interviewing are not always attainable. Sometimes, researchers must make do with whatever is available. For example, in Sri Lanka, there was wide variation in the sites for focus groups with schoolchildren held for the purpose of exploring concepts of mental health and mental health programming. Researchers used whatever space was available in the school or in the schoolyard and managed some degree of privacy by asking curious nonparticipants to leave the area.

EXAMPLE 2.8

ENSURING PRIVACY AND CONFIDENTIALITY IN FOCUSED GROUP
INTERVIEWING: INTERVIEWING SCHOOLCHILDREN IN SRI LANKA

In one instance, researchers held a meeting in a public school run by Catholic nuns. Adolescent girls were eager to talk until researchers probed the topic of relationships with boys. The girls advised the researchers that one of the nuns had entered the library and was seated at a distance reading. The girls were reluctant to disclose any information, and researchers had to ask the nun to leave in order to continue the conversation (B. K. Nastasi, personal communication, March 1998).

IDENTIFYING AND TRAINING FACILITATORS

> *Basic Skills for Group Interviewers*
>
> - Fieldwork skills
> - Knowledge of interviewing
> - Group facilitation and management skills
> - Survey research technique

Informal group interviewing in community or other naturalistic settings requires good ethnographic fieldwork skills.
Ethnographic skills (see Books 1 and 2) are defined here as

- The ability to become integrated into the field setting
- The skills to conduct participant observation
- The ability to synthesize qualitative data and formulate questions spontaneously in the field
- Being able to ask questions in a group setting as if one were a
  member of the group while still eliciting more or less satisfac-
  tory answers
- The ability to mentally (and physically) record responses in
  the field so that they can be recalled and reconstructed later
- Experience in using appropriate equipment for recording ethnographic data

Formal focus group interviewers should have the same
ethnographic interviewing skills used in informal interviews. Although they will need to follow their open-ended
interview schedule instead of improvising questions on the
spot, they also must use probes, new questions, and other
techniques to stimulate participants to talk. They also must
retain very large amounts of qualitative information, be
able to sift through it quickly, and organize it spontaneously
so as to improve or add to the existing interview schedule
as situations require.

Good group facilitation skills are a real advantage for any
focus group leader because formal focus groups must be
directed and managed purposefully. The focus group leader
should be able to help group members to meet one another
and build a degree of trust and group identity. An experienced facilitator can help each respondent see that his or
her views are important and can create opportunities for
each respondent to participate.

Group leaders must control individuals who are confrontational, dominating, or overly opinioned or emotional; they also must prevent the group from getting distracted from the topic of discussion and refocus participants who decide to talk with one another rather than focus on the topic.

Finally, formal focus group facilitators can benefit from experience in survey research. As part of their interviewing responsibility, they may be expected to collect systematically some numerical or demographic data—such as age, residence, gender, ethnicity, marital status, or level of formal education—from each member of the focus group. It is often useful to collect such data from participants just prior to the beginning of a group session. Facilitators with some survey research experience know why it is important to make sure that the data are collected from each member; they are familiar with how forms used to collect such data are constructed and should review the forms before the session is over to make sure that the information is complete.

Who Can Best Run
Your Focus Groups?

The best candidates to facilitate formal focus groups are those with whom the respondents feel comfortable and confident enough to express their opinions easily. It is important to consider in advance who these candidates might be. Should they be ethnographically trained researchers or project lead investigators, or not? If not, what kind of experience should they have? Should they be of the same age or ethnic group as the participants? How much prior experience should they have had with the subject matter in order to be able to ask good questions while empathizing with the respondents? Should a special kind of facilitator be chosen if the topic of discussion is an illegal activity? Should the facilitator have the same professional credentials as the respondents—for example, is it better to select someone with teaching experience and a degree to conduct focused group interviews with educators? Should there be co-facilitators? If so, how should they be chosen so that they complement one another, and how should they work together?

Good formal focus group facilitators are individuals who

- Have language skills that match those of the respondents
- Demonstrate that they can function well in a group setting
- Have no strong opinions about the topic in question, or who can withhold their opinions during the group's discussions
- Do not wish to use focus groups as a platform for their own views
- Are good listeners
- Have conceptual skills and can demonstrate that they can summarize the suggestions and ideas of group members in a manner consistent with what those individuals have said
- Are members of the target population

It is always an advantage if lead or staff researchers have these characteristics. Focus group facilitators with more open-ended research skills and greater knowledge of the substantive area to be explored will be able to obtain more information. The example below shows how knowledgeable lay people possessing these characteristics can be used as group interviewers.

EXAMPLE 2.9

TRAINING NONETHNOGRAPHERS TO CONDUCT QUALITATIVE ASSESSMENTS FOR
IMPROVEMENT OF RURAL NUTRITIONAL SERVICES AND GROWTH MONITORING

Husaini, Satoto, and Karyadi (1992) illustrate ways in which nonethnographers can
be trained to conduct qualitative assessments to improve capacity for growth monitoring and improvement of nutritional services. In their study, regional nutritionists
were trained for 1 week to collect data using rapid assessment procedures (RAP).
Focus group interviews were held with three groups:

1. Mothers with children under 3 years, chosen randomly from those visiting
   the center on that day
2. Kadres (health volunteers) active on the day of the interviewing
3. Key people in each village, including heads of subvillages and hamlets,
   religious leaders, women of the family welfare movement, and members of
   the village community welfare movement

Information focused on knowledge, beliefs, attitudes, and practices in monthly
weighing, use of health outpost (Posyandu) services, breast feeding and infant
feeding, and benefits provided by the Posyandu for people attending. Focus group
sessions lasted 1½ hours. Each meeting was guided by two nutritionists, one facilitating and the other recording. Focus group data demonstrated the existence of
important variations across communities in circumstances of service, level of volun-
teerism, protocols for weighing and recording, administration of vitamins, availability of counseling, role of family, and frequency of visits. These data were taken into
consideration in the creation of a program for improvement of local outpost services
(Husaini et al., 1992).

Rather than hiring outside facilitators, project researchers should take the opportunity whenever possible to
conduct their own formal focus group interviews, because
they are the individuals most familiar with what information needs to be obtained from the interview. Like any other
facilitator, they should use the opportunity to maximize the
acquisition of information while minimizing any unin-
tended effort to influence the results of discussion. Using
the researchers themselves to conduct focus group inter-

views also limits the number of focus group leaders, which, in turn, reduces variations in results stemming from interviewer difference.

Focused group interviews are often conducted in multilingual, cross-cultural, or cross-national settings, where one or more members of the research team do not understand the local language. Here, the research team must work together to construct appropriate questions in the local language, consistent with local cultural beliefs and practices and with the developmental stage of the participants. Prior ethnographic experience, coupled with cross-cultural teamwork, is helpful in such situations, as is the identification of a good translator. The complicated nature of the translation process should not be underestimated. At best, it involves joint decision making about the terms and concepts to be used in the project, or at least paying careful attention to how such terms and concepts are translated into local language so that all researchers/interviewers understand the basic principles and questions of the research. The following examples illustrate this process.

EXAMPLE 2.10

CROSS-CULTURAL COLLABORATION TO ENSURE CROSS-NATIONAL
TRANSFERABILITY OF LANGUAGE AND CONCEPTS

Nastasi and her colleagues conducted focus group interviews with middle school children in central Sri Lanka. The team included a Sri Lankan child psychiatrist and a professor of education. The team met together to formulate questions appropriate for the cultural setting and age of the children. In addition to translating questions from English to Tamil and Sinhala, the researchers had to translate language use from theoretical constructs to lay language, and from adult to children's language usages. This transformation occurred not only in the formulation phase but also in the field, as results were translated from Tamil and Sinhala, which generated still more questions from English-only researchers. These were then translated back into either of the two local languages in a style appropriate for the group (B. K. Nastasi, personal communication, 1998).

Responsibilities of Facilitators

It is the responsibility of the facilitator to cover the important questions in sequence, to remember group responses, and to use the information during the group session to improve the question sequence. One facilitator is needed to run an average-sized focus group of about 5 to 15 members. Usually, a single facilitator is better than two for a focus group of this size because the flow of questioning can be lost unless two facilitators are able to work together with a high degree of empathy and coordination.

The focus group facilitator has several key responsibilities. She or he must

- Keep the discussion on topic.
- Ensure that the topics to be addressed in the group are culturally acceptable for the majority of the group members.
- Help individuals in the group to avoid extremely personal disclosures that they might regret later.
- Make sure that the focus group is not a therapy group.
- Make sure that every participant in the group has an opportunity to speak as well as to listen.

Cross Reference: Book 1, Chapter 1, includes guidelines for use of audiovisual equipment

Facilitators need a recording partner to take notes using a computer, notebook, newsprint (or flipchart or white/blackboard), audiotape recorder, video camera, or other locally available recording device. The recorder also should know as much about the topic as the facilitator because he or she must recognize what is important to record. Training in knowing *what* to record applies—even though the rule of thumb is to record everything, or at least as much as possible—regardless of modes of recording. Later in this chapter, we will discuss types of data collected in the focus group setting and how to record the important points.

The facilitators should practice in advance in order to avoid reinforcing one point of view or set of comments over another. They should be able to recognize that some people may feel more comfortable elaborating on their views in public than others and may be able to express themselves more effectively. Facilitators can help participants expand upon their ideas by using interviewing techniques such as probes, repeated statements, or statements such as "Can you explain a little bit more about what you mean?" "Can you define the term you just used, so that others can understand it a bit more clearly?" or "Could you given an example of what you mean?"

CONDUCTING A FOCUSED GROUP INTERVIEW

Getting Started

In opening the focus group discussion, the facilitator should make sure to

- Explain the purpose of the group discussion, why participants have been selected or invited, and why they are important to the project
- Explain the roles of the facilitator and the recorder(s)
- Ask permission to audio- or videotape
- Have everyone introduce themselves at the beginning
- Explain the ground rules for the discussion:
  —Everyone should participate
  —All ideas are equally valid
  —There are no right or wrong answers
  —Each person's view should be heard and respected

Participants should be told that "no one wins" in a focus group. Participants are free to respond to and disagree with the ideas or opinions of another group member; disagreement is helpful, but it should be presented with respect or as an alternative viewpoint rather than as a way to discredit the ideas of others.

Handling Problematic Group Behaviors

To make sure that groups run smoothly, focus group facilitators need to use group process skills to troubleshoot or prevent problems that can arise in any small group. Some typical problems and their solutions are:

Problem	Solution
Some members of the group do not speak.	The facilitator calls on each group member one by one, repeating the question or someone else's response. He or she makes sure to ask individuals who have not contributed, "What do you think about X?"
Some members of the group speak too much.	The facilitator asks those individuals to wait for their turn, to "hold their idea" for a moment, or to wait until others have had an opportunity to speak.
One group member dominates the conversation by speaking too often, too loudly, for too long, or in a coercive or intimidating manner.	The facilitator reminds the group of the ground rules and the purpose of the focus group. If the offending individual does not understand or change behavior, the facilitator asks the participant directly to conform to the ground rules, either during the group session or during a break.
Group members talk to people next to them but not with the group.	The facilitator first determines the cause of the problem: for example, the group may be too big; some participants may feel uncomfortable speaking in a large group; respondents may not have received enough opportunity to express their opinions; the conversation may be difficult to follow; or some groups may not be able to understand the way that others express themselves. Some participants may feel uncomfortable with a subtopic, or they may disagree with what someone said but feel uneasy saying so in public. The facilitator should take a few moments to observe and discuss with the individuals what the problem is. A solution then can be devised.

Problem	Solution
Group members begin to take sides on an issue.	The facilitator reminds group members that everyone's opinion is valued and that differences of opinion are important as opportunities for learning. The facilitator encourages participants to state their opinions and to discuss and debate different points of view, but to avoid open conflict, because it can divide a group and preclude further open discussion, which disrupts the intention of the focus group.
Group discussion diverges from the interview focus.	The facilitator returns group members to the topic with a polite reminder and/or a shift in questioning. If group members do not wish to return to the topic scheduled for discussion right away, they can be invited to postpone the new topic until after the session is over, at which point they can remain and continue to discuss the new topic for as long as they wish. Divergence can happen very quickly. Facilitators should exercise care when letting discussion flow, even if they are trying to avoid offending respondents by cutting off discussion. The facilitator should remember that each formal focus group interview member was selected because he or she was known to have experience and opinions on the topic to be discussed, and that because of their expertise, they are receiving incentives for their participation.
Participants have ideas relevant to the topic, but either have not thought them out clearly or cannot express themselves well.	Facilitators probe by asking additional questions but avoid suggesting likely extensions of the respondent's thoughts. Some people work best from the basis of concrete examples; facilitators can ask such respondents to give some examples of what they mean and then question them for clarity. Facilitators can also ask other group members to describe similar situations that may stimulate the thoughts of the struggling group member.

Troubleshooting in the Field

Even with the best preparation, a number of unanticipated challenges and problems can occur in the field. Some of the most common problems with which we we are familiar are the following:

- No one arrives.
- Some people are late.
- Only half of those invited show up.
- Unexpected problems occur at the site.

People do not arrive. There are many reasons for "no-shows." There could be a mistake in the address, an accident or other problem with transportation, failure to receive information about the location of the group meeting, unanticipated resistance by participants to the idea of a group session or to the facilitators, or insufficient understanding of the purpose of the group session. Because definitions of "lateness" vary from one community to another, one rule of thumb is to wait a full hour to make sure that respondents have not encountered any unforeseen difficulties in reaching the meeting. The best strategy is to assume that there has been a misunderstanding. If no one arrives, it is imperative to check with key informants and respondents the next day to determine what has caused the misunderstanding and reschedule the event, taking the feedback into consideration.

Some of the invited participants are late. The late arrival of some group members disrupts a formal focus group. We advise determining standard arrival times in the groups with whom the focus group is to be conducted. If 15 minutes to 30 minutes delay in starting is the standard cultural practice, organizers can plan to delay the start of the focus group for 30 minutes and serve food or schedule a socializing time to precede the formal start of the interview session. Whether those respondents who arrive after the group begins are allowed to join the group depends on their lateness of arrival and the discretion of the facilitator. We suggest that those who arrive a few minutes late can join the group; those who arrive 15 minutes or more after the group begins may be asked to wait to join the next group. It is important to keep in mind that many factors can prevent a group member from arriving at a focus group session on time, and to plan a makeup session if possible.

Fewer than half of those invited come to the group session. If the research design depends on the interaction of the full complement of participants, the facilitator should ask those who did come to reschedule. Facilitators whose designs allow them to be more flexible can hold the focus group with the smaller sample of participants and reschedule a second group session with the remainder of the group at another time.

There are logistical difficulties at the interview site. Any number of problems can occur, such as faulty or missing equipment, inappropriate room size or furniture, changed location, broken heating or air conditioning, late arrival of food or drink, or finding that someone else is using the interview room for another purpose. There also can be unanticipated and unacceptable background noise at the interview site. The best solution to these problems is to arrive early enough to address any such problem in advance of the session.

Perhaps the best advice for focus group organizers is to maintain flexibility and good humor, be assertive in requesting needed resources, and recognize that there are always at least two or three ways to solve a problem. Most people do

Key point

not mind working in less than ideal circumstances for a short period of time if the facilitators and other research team members are pleasant, supportive, and accommodating.

HOW TO ASK QUESTIONS IN A FOCUSED GROUP INTERVIEW

Focused group interviews are often described as "qualitative data," meaning that they generate verbal (or sometimes written) responses to open-ended interview questions. But many different types of data can be collected from a group through an interview format. Focused group interviews, whether informal or formal, make most frequent use of open-ended questions when the issues to be explored are not very well understood and the facilitators would like to provide the broadest possible latitude for response. It is very important for facilitators, other researchers, and recorders to meet beforehand to determine the core questions. For a 90-minute group interview, five to seven core questions are sufficient. We suggest beginning the discussion with the focal topic rather than the background context questions.

EXAMPLE 2.11

FOCUS GROUP QUESTIONS WITH SERVICE PROVIDERS
CONCERNED WITH ALZHEIMER'S DISEASE

In a focus group session researchers Schensul and Wetle organized with health care providers for patients with Alzheimer's disease, we asked three major questions:

1. What are the main symptoms of dementia?
2. Which of these symptoms are more important in reporting and diagnosing Alzheimer's disease?
3. What similarities and differences have you observed in assessing patients of different ethnic groups and seeing them clinically?

In our 1-hour discussions with service providers about symptoms of Alzheimer's disease, we asked them to list as a group the major symptoms of dementia and then to discuss the meaning and importance of each one in relation to Alzheimer's disease. Then, we went on to discuss their observations and experiences serving Puerto Rican patients and families with symptoms of dementia. Toward the end, we asked them to compare their experiences with families across the ethnic spectrum. Our purpose in asking this question was to obtain more information about their relative exposure to Puerto Rican families and their beliefs and attitudes about Puerto Rican seniors and dementia in comparison to other families (Schensul, Torres, & Wetle, 1994).

In addition to the core questions, facilitators used a number of probes and additional questions intended to help clarify or elaborate on participants' responses. For example, in relation to the first question, we asked for a definition of dementias, why some of the symptoms listed were related to dementia, and whether some of the items on the list could be collapsed or combined with others. The second question led to our request for a medical definition of Alzheimer's disease (AD), as well as to additional questions about difficulty in diagnosis and available treatments or strategies for management of symptoms of AD dementia. The third question produced the observation that most patients served by the health care providers were not Puerto Rican. This offered facilitators the opportunity to raise questions about barriers to symptom identification and reporting among Puerto Rican families.

Subquestions or areas of discussion such as these can be identified in advance. Facilitators should list the subquestions or areas of exploration that they believe to be important and then raise these questions in the course of the discussion. In addition, facilitators should be alert to the possibility of asking additional clarifying questions based on the content of the discussion. The more familiar the facilitators are with the topic, the more likely they are to ask good questions on topics they had not anticipated but which arose in the course of discussion.

As the example above illustrates, we advocate organizing focus groups around a logical sequence of questioning in which facilitators go directly to the primary subject matter, and then explore contextual factors. For example:

- What is diabetes? What are the causes? How do you get it?
- How do you know when you have diabetes?
- Is it preventable? What can you do to prevent it?
- Of the list of things you have suggested to prevent it, which are the easiest to do?
- Why?
- Which are the most difficult to do? Why?
- What will help people to identify the symptoms of diabetes and report them to their clinic or doctor?

The sequence just portrayed moves from the problem to factors that contribute to it, and then to what people perceive to be things they can and cannot do to report or prevent it. It concludes with facilitators and barriers to reporting. A similar sequence eliciting perceptions of gender in young women might begin with the following:

- What are some differences between girls and boys? (Probes)
- What are some similarities between girls and boys? (Probes)

These can be listed on a flipchart or newsprint and then further discussed in the focus group as follows:

- What do you like about being a girl?
- What don't you like about being a girl?

Characteristics of Good
Focus Group Questions

As is the case with surveys, questionnaires, or any interview, the open-ended questions used in focus groups should not be vague, leading, or misleading. Some examples of such questions are the following:

■ *Leading* (in a focus group with master teaching artists on instruction in elementary school classrooms): "Don't you think that artists should be allowed to work independently with children in the classroom?"

■ *Vague* (in a focus group to elicit children's activities): "What kinds of things do boys and girls do during the day?"

■ *Misleading* (in a focus group with parents to identify their concerns about adolescent risks): "What types of violence do you think teenagers in this neighborhood may be exposed to?"

Questions should not be phrased in the negative. They can be framed to solicit an individual/personal response, such as "Did you ever use drugs with your friends?" or to elicit an opinion about the reference group, such as "Do people your age (or your friends) ever use drugs?" In summary, focus group questions should permit people to describe what they do, why they do these things, and how they feel about them. Facilitators should be genuinely curious about the responses and should not convey in words, gestures, or facial expressions whether they value one response or even one style of response over another. Facilitators also should allow respondents a few minutes to write down or to reflect upon their responses, because not all participants respond at the same rate.

Elicitation techniques are generally used with individual respondents. They can also be used as techniques for stimulating group dialogue. For example, group "freelisting" of

Cross Reference: See Book 2, Chapters 6, 7, and 8, for more detailed discussion of these methods

Cross Reference: See Chapter 3 in this book for a discussion of elicitation techniques

cultural domains, such as children's activities, drug para-phernalia, or beliefs about the cause and prevention of diabetes, can provoke interesting discussion and ethno-graphic data with respect to whether or not items belong in the domain. Group sorting, in which participants are asked to discuss and organize items into predetermined catego-ries, generates similar ethnographic data regarding differ-ences and similarities in the way in which items in a cultural domain are grouped, and how group members manage differences of opinion.

EXAMPLE 2.12   ➤•➤•➤

FREELISTING, SORTING, AND SCALING THE MEANING OF VIOLENT BEHAVIORS

In 1995, action researchers Allison Bingham and Jean Schensul worked with a vio-lence prevention coalition in a suburban town to prevent the acceleration of violent behavior in several target communities. The first agreed-upon step was to understand differences in the meaning of violence in the community. In a freelist exercise, a broad diversity of residents working in small groups identified behaviors that they consid-ered to be somewhat violent to very violent. These behaviors (a total of approximately 26) were listed and written, one to a card. The items included, for example, speaking loudly as a group in front of someone's house, loud criticism of someone in public, hitting with a belt, shooting, and killing someone intentionally. The second step in-volved determining where the areas of agreement and disagreement lay in the defi-nition of violence. At the next meeting of the coalition, small groups were asked to discuss and agree on the placement of each of the items on a matrix of degree of violence by degree of acceptability. Each group had to decide where the behavior should be placed on a 5-point horizontal Likert scale from *not violent* to *very violent,* and on a 5-point vertical scale arranged from *acceptable* to *not acceptable.* The four extremes were very violent-very acceptable, very violent-very *un*acceptable, not violent-*un*acceptable, and not violent-very acceptable. The conversation was docu-mented in writing and on audiotape with the permission of all of the participants and treated as text data for coding purposes. The exercise produced valuable infor-mation on the ways in which participants viewed behaviors and why they defined them as violent. Furthermore, it provided information on the reasons behind differ-ential tolerance of behavior.

➤•➤•➤

Maps can be used in much the same way to promote group discussion about how and why social phenomena are arranged in space and to what degree there is group consensus regarding placement. In an open-ended approach to social geography, participants are given a map of a socio-geographic space, such as a neighborhood, and asked to place on the map locations where the social events that are the subject of the research occur. In Hartford, Connecticut, for example, teenagers were given a map of a neighborhood and asked to identify locations where children play together; where teenagers hang out, and what they do in those locations; and the ethnic composition of the groups to be found in each location. Discussions provided a picture of age and ethnic differentiation in the use of neighborhood open or public spaces as well as typical types of public activities in this neighborhood. In another example, teenagers were asked to identify locations where billboards promoted the use of alcohol among young adults, and then to discuss why billboards were concentrated in one geographic area versus another.

Cross Reference: See Book 4, Chapter 2, for information about social mapping and the arrangement of social variables in space

Collage, drawing, and other creative ways of producing conversation are useful techniques for initiating focused group discussions, especially with children. Children and inexperienced adult speakers often enjoy the opportunity to draw their subject matter or portray it visually in other ways. Researchers can ask them to draw or produce a collage based on found objects, miscellaneous materials, or magazine pictures that shows the researchers their interpretation of the research topic. The participants are told that they must present and then discuss the meaning of their collage with the group. The presentation and discussion are recorded and, together with the collages, constitute the basis for later text analysis. At the time of this writing, an artist in New York has organized an installation around this theme. He took photographs of his topic and invited selected respondents to respond to his work in groups. The responses were superimposed on glass overlaying the photographs and thus were integrated into the presentation. He calls his installation "focus group photography."

Focus groups also can be used productively to collect data on social relations. Researchers can show an organizational chart (an "organogram") to a group of respondents and then ask its members to describe and discuss the relationships among components or departments. To obtain information about personal relationships, such as friendship, respondents can be given a diagram showing themselves in the middle, surrounded by circles. They can then be asked to fill in the circles with the first or fictive names of their closest personal friends. In focused group discussion, they can then compare the size of their personal friendship networks and the ways in which they define close personal friends. Such discussions reveal important ethnographic data about social relations in their community.

Group interviews can also be used to collect numerical data that demonstrate patterns; these patterns can then be discussed with the group, producing interesting ethnographic data.

EXAMPLE 2.13

COLLECTING NUMERICAL DATA THROUGH
SYSTEMATIC FOCUS GROUP INTERVIEWS

Seven groups of young adult Sri Lankan women were given a list of sex behaviors and asked to check which were "sex" and which were "risky sex." When each individual in each group had completed the task, they handed the exercise sheets to the focus group facilitator. The facilitator then asked each group to do the same exercise together and to discover and discuss their differences of opinion for each. The discussion was documented. The exercise was then repeated with groups of males of the same age group. Differences between male and female responses were noted in the text data and in the quantitative responses, and presented to a mixed group of young men and women for discussion of the differences (Nastasi et al., 1998).

══•══•══

The data can also be collected in the context of a group discussion, where each individual provides the same information, which is then tabulated so that everyone can see the distribution of responses. Such data may be biased by "group effects" or group pressure. However, certain kinds of data (closer to "facts") are less likely to be biased by group influence than others and may even promote more accurate self-revelation or reporting. Researchers must decide whether the data they wish to obtain from each individual is subject to response bias, and whether they would like to collect it prior to, during, or after a group discussion.

 **EXAMPLE 2.14**

AVOIDING GROUP BIAS IN THE REPORTING OF SENSITIVE DATA

Community reproductive health educators met with a group of 12 Latina women to discuss contraceptive choice. They knew from prior research in that community that more than 50% of women of childbearing age (under the age of 45) had been sterilized. During the discussion of contraceptive alternatives, one of the facilitators asked if any of the women had considered sterilization as a contraceptive measure. When the response was yes, the facilitator asked a series of questions, prepared before the session, about the circumstances of sterilization, such as where; by whom; when (immediately after the birth, 1 month later, more than 6 months later); how many live births each woman had; size of household; occupational status then and now; and so on. These data were summarized in the form of "yes/no" on a chart developed in a seemingly spontaneous manner during the session. Researchers had numerical or potentially numerical data for each participant that were entered into a quantitative, individual database. Participants, viewing the data in front of them, had a convincing portrayal of the range of variation in the sterilization experience. Discussion of this range produced text data on behaviors and attitudes with respect to sterilization in this ethnic group (Jean Schensul, fieldnotes, 1985).

It is important to remember that numerical data obtained in this way can be used only descriptively. They can never be treated as representative of the whole population from which focus group members were selected. Only studies using all members of a population or a random sample from all members are appropriate for this purpose. Focus group data should never be treated as if they are obtained from a random sample of respondents.

Cross Reference:
See Books 1 and 2 for discussions of sampling procedures

RECORDING DATA FOR FOCUSED GROUP INTERVIEWS

It is critically important to record accurately and completely what is said in a focused group interview. If recording is not understandable or complete, valuable information can be misinterpreted, incompletely remembered, or lost. Because each method of recording interview data has advantages and disadvantages, we would recommend that you consider using at least two techniques simultaneously to make sure that you capture everything of importance. Some optional combinations are videotaping and written observations; audiotaping and written observations; videotaping and recording group contributions in shorthand notes or brainstorming lists on newsprint pads; or having two observers record their observations in writing at the same time.

Using Notepads/Notebooks in the Field

When recording in a natural setting, ethnographers prefer to use unobtrusive means of recording, such as a small notebook, file cards, scrap paper, or the backs of letters or notes. Recorders in more formal focused interview settings can use more conspicuous materials to record and write up their fieldnotes by hand, because these activities are clearly designed to collect information on specific topics. As with newsprint records, other written records based on the observations of individual recorders will be limited in terms of documenting the "dialogue" among focus group participants simply because the recorder cannot make the observations, listen to the discussions, and write them down quickly enough to capture them in a comprehensive way. This is why we suggest supplementing fieldnotes in focus group settings with audiovisual forms of data collection.

Recording Focus Group Conversations Directly Into a Computer as Text Data

Formal focus group data can be recorded directly into a computer. Because these groups are scheduled in advance and located in a specific site in the community, it is much easier for recorders to locate themselves in a comfortable location before the interview starts, find out where to plug in their portable computers, and then record the conversation (and their own observations) as the interview takes place. Recorders who use computers in such settings are sometimes referred to as "rapporteurs." This term conveys the idea that everything that every participant says is worth recording permanently, word for word, and that all of the materials will be summarized and used. If the focus group team decides that portable computers can be used, the following conventions should be observed:

- The recorder/rapporteur should be introduced.
- The importance of the computer in the interview situation should be noted.
- The computer should have a relatively quiet keyboard so as not to interfere with the discussion.
- If the computer is portable, it should be plugged in so that no time is lost if the battery dies.
- Plug locations should be identified in advance to make sure that the computer can be set up in a location where it is

comfortable for the recorder to enter data, and where the recorder can hear everything being discussed.

■ Data should be saved automatically every five minutes on the computer's hard drive and backed up at the same time on a portable disk to avoid inadvertent data loss.

Newspaper Pads or Flip Charts

Typically, recorders work with facilitators to record the main individual or group responses to a question. The newsprint is purchased in large pads and hung on an easel within easy viewing of all group members. The recorder writes the main ideas on the newsprint with a Magic Marker and asks the group to verify that what is written reflects what the speakers intended. Recording ideas and suggestions on newsprint provides immediate feedback and recall to group participants, and it may encourage them to think of new things or to recognize and discuss differences of opinion. Use of newsprint also has the advantage of immediate feedback to the group, and it creates a democratic process in which all respondents have access to the "data" as they emerge from the group.

Individual contributions to the conversation may vary considerably. Listing them on newsprint offers both the facilitator and the participants an opportunity to see directly where differences of opinion lie and to address them right away. Finally, the questions asked of each group member may require numerical (or categorical) responses, such as "How old are you?" or "How many times did you shop in a large supermarket in the past week?" A question to each group member calling for a categorical response—which could also be counted—might be "Did you use any drug of any kind in the past month?" In this case, the response would be "yes," "no," or "don't remember." The frequency of these "countable" responses, if placed on newsprint, could be enumerated during the meeting for immediate discussion.

> **To use newsprint, you need the following equipment:**
>
> ■ One or more newsprint stands that have been checked in advance to make sure
>   — They will fit the specific newsprint pads you have
>   — They do not fall down easily when the recorder is writing.
> ■ At least two newsprint pads with pages that can be easily detached.
> ■ Masking tape or other tape that does not destroy paint or wallpaper, for hanging up newsprint sheets.
> ■ Four new markers of different colors.

Recorders who like to use newsprint should supplement their notes with some other form of recording—either direct observation with written notes, or audiotaping—because the quality and complexity of the dialogue among participants cannot be captured on newsprint alone. Newsprint lends itself to shorthand summaries, not detailed notes of conversations; and the recorder usually cannot write fast enough on newsprint to capture all of the important information. In addition, newsprint pads are relatively expensive, and taking detailed notes can mean using many pages. Using notebooks or audiotapes also avoids the "wallpaper problem"—having to hang too many newsprint sheets around the focus group discussion space. Also, having data written on many sheets of newsprint rather than in small notebooks, notepads, or computer files is awkward to analyze, especially in a small office space!

Audiotaping

Audiotaped focused group discussions can be used very effectively to supplement other forms of recording group interviews and discussions. They capture verbatim the words and emotions of the respondents, the exchanges among respondents, new questions and probes that facilitators introduce to obtain additional information, and the sequence of questioning occurring in the session. If sessions are held in languages different from the first languages of the researchers, audiotaping captures the "flavor" of the language, the sound of the words, and their context and meanings in ways that are difficult to match with written notes alone.

It is always best to transcribe audiotaped sessions as quickly as possible after the session takes place. The most efficient (although not always the most popular) way for transcription and translation to take place is for the facilitator(s) or session recorders to do it because they were directly involved with the session and can take from the tapes exactly what they need to complement their fieldnotes. Facilitators and session recorders can also **log the tapes** while they are listening to them and comparing them to the fieldnotes. Logging involves tagging or noting the location of a segment on the tape by time or other locational unit and topic, and then recording the location in a log or notebook. Several verbatim lines from the tape or tape transcript are entered at the beginning and at the end, as well as a description of the content. In this way, other researchers can return to specific sections of a tape to retrieve information without having to listen to the entire tape once again. If these methods cannot be used, the next best strategy is to build into the project budget funds for someone else to transcribe and translate all tapes from beginning to end.

Definition: Logging tapes means marking them so that specific content can be located

Using audiotapes requires you to

■ Check your equipment beforehand to make sure it works
■ Make sure that you have enough audiotapes to cover the entire span of the group discussion (preferably 90 to 120 minutes on a tape)

- Make sure that your recorder knows how to use the tape recorder
- Visit the location beforehand to locate the placement of the microphones if they are external to the tape recorder
- Make sure that you put new batteries in your tape recorder before the session or that you have located a source of electrical current that accommodates your cord
- Avoid using inexpensive, small, hand-held tape recorders or mini-tape recorders for focused group interviews, because their sound quality usually is poor, and they break easily

Notwithstanding these rules of thumb, *researchers should not depend on audiotaping as the sole means of recording unless there are no other options,* because so much can go wrong, resulting in the loss of important data. Even the best audiotape recorder with a directional microphone has difficulty clearly recording a group discussion in which people speak simultaneously or interrupt one another. Background noise can impair sound quality. The best microphones have to be moved to record all the speakers as they speak. Over time, people can forget to move the mike from one site to another around a large table. It is even more challenging if the group discussion takes place in a home, where the noise levels and acoustical quality of the space are uncontrollable. Controversial points, areas of disagreement, and other moments when more than one participant at a time speaks can be lost to the tape recorder. Unless the people operating the recorders have experience with the equipment, they may not recognize when the tapes are filled and need to be replaced. All too often, researchers discover that only part of the session was recorded, the tape ran out and was not replaced, the machine was never turned on, or it broke during the recording period. Experience and close observation during the session can help to prevent these technical problems.

Key point

Videotaping

Cross Reference: See Book 3, Chapter 1, for more information on audiovisual techniques for data collection

Videotaping is a more effective means of recording individual comments and group interaction than audiotaping—although the same cautions about use of equipment that we listed for audiotaping also hold true for videotaping. The use of videotape is consistent with one of the primary objectives of the focused group interview: to capture the exchanges of ideas and opinions of group members in a naturalistic setting. Provided that the group is small enough so that every participant can be included in group discussions, virtually everything that occurs in the group can be recorded in sight, sound, and color.

It is always best to ask a skilled video recorder to film focused group interviews. Skilled recorders will know when to focus the camera on an individual, on two or more people in discussion, or on the entire group; when to fade in and out, and how to ensure that the words of the participants are fully and audibly captured on tape. The words of the speakers must be clearly audible for the videotape to be useful to the focus group researcher. Even experienced documenters must still be trained to recognize which information in the interview is most important. Camera personnel should be involved with the rest of the focus group research team in discussions about the interview topic(s), the flow of the interview, and the information desired.

Lead researchers should decide with camera personnel exactly when they should film group discussion versus a respondent's single contribution to the topic. For novice film recorders, practice sessions in which research team members or volunteers role play focus group sessions can be very helpful. If you plan to use videotape, you will need the following:

> *List of Equipment or Supplies*
> *Needed for Videotaping:*
>
> ■ One or more video cameras with film cartridges
>   (e.g., for shooting individuals and the entire group
>   from different angles)
> ■ Tripods
> ■ Portable microphones
> ■ Lighting equipment (nonessential)

In earlier sections of this chapter, we listed different techniques for recording focused group interview data, what equipment to bring, and how to check it. Following is a list of other materials you should have prepared prior to conducting a focus group session.

> *Focus Group Checklist*
>
> _____ List of questions to be asked
> _____ List of participants
> _____ Name tags for participants
> _____ Notebook, portable computer, audio or video
>   equipment (use recorder checklists to be sure you
>   have everything you need)
> _____ Video tripod
> _____ Incentives for participants
> _____ Pens and markers
> _____ Newsprint stand and newsprint pad
> _____ Paper and pencil for participants
> _____ Food and drinks of your choice
> _____ Baby-sitting/child care equipment

VALIDITY AND RELIABILITY[3]

Regardless of how formally or informally they are organized, inquiry and focus groups generally are almost always used either for explorative or project development purposes, or to complement other forms of ethnographic data collection. Focused group interview data are almost always qualitative. Researchers do not expect the same questions asked in different group settings to produce the same responses; indeed, it may be preferable that they produce different responses so that the researchers can gain a rounded understanding of the full range of responses within the target population. For these reasons, the concepts of validity and reliability, critical to all scientific research, have different meanings when applied to ethnographic focus group data as compared to quantitative data and experimental research. In this section, we will discuss the meaning of these terms as applied to ethnographic data obtained from groups rather than individuals.

Validity

Definition: Validity is a measure of fit between researcher and respondent perceptions and meanings, or between data collection procedures and what they purport to collect

Validity is concerned with accuracy of findings. It refers to "the degree to which the procedure really measures what it proposes to measure" (Krueger, 1988, p. 41), or the degree to which responses are a valid reflection of how participants felt and thought about the topic (Krueger, 1998). Validity also depends on the appropriateness of the research design for the context of the study and question for which it is being used. If a focus group is inappropriate to use in the culture or context of the research, the results will not be valid. Establishing validity requires researchers to

- Determine the extent to which conclusions effectively represent empirical reality
- Assess whether constructs devised by researchers represent or measure the categories of human experience that occur

There are two kinds of validity: internal and external. *Internal validity* refers to the extent to which scientific observations generate data and measurements that authentically represent some reality—for example, the way in which a given group of people views its world. *External validity* refers to the degree to which such representations can be compared legitimately across groups, as well as the extent to which one group or a sample of groups is representative of an entire population.

Validity can be enhanced in group interviewing by

- Pilot testing the questions to make sure that participants understand them
- Taking the advice of participants in creating a welcoming environment that fosters sharing and discussion
- Using culturally appropriate facilitators—people whom respondents trust or with whom they feel comfortable
- Situating the focus group in an appropriate location
- Clarifying ambiguity in questions and interim interpretations
- Discussing research results with participants for interpretive comments before they are published or disseminated

Reliability addresses whether the results of a study can be duplicated. Reliability is a lesser concern in ethnographic research, and especially in focused group interviews, because these interviews are specifically meant to be exploratory. Duplication of results across groups is not the desired outcome of focused group interviews. There is good reason to avoid lengthy discussions of reliability in focused group interviews, because they are not meant to reflect stability or generalizability. Rather, the intention of these interviews is to provide exploratory information leading to theory formulation, more valid instrument development, and explanation of quantitative results. Thus, for this form of research, differences are more important than similarities. But careful training of interviewers, team interviewing, rigorous notes and audiovisual documentation, and thought given in advance to the structure of the questions to be used in the group interview can go a long way toward ensuring that other researchers could approximate the research process (although not necessarily the results). Using other data to

Definition: Reliability concerns whether or not a study can be replicated

confirm the results of focused group interviews is another way of ensuring reliability of results. Following are examples of ways in which two researchers addressed issues of reliability and validity in their field settings.

EXAMPLE 2.15

IDENTIFYING INTRAGROUP DIFFERENCES IN
VIEWS OF FAMILY PLANNING IN CAMEROON

Paul Nkwi, an anthropologist at the University of Yaounde, Cameroon, studied people's perceptions of family planning. He and his research team worked in four communities, using a combination of participant observation, in-depth interviews, a questionnaire, and focus groups. They conducted nine focus groups that were stratified by gender and age (12 to 19, 20 to 35, 36 to 49, and 50 and over) and one mixed group by gender and age in which they examined the following topics:

- Community development
- Resistance to family planning
- Cultural and economic factors that could be used to promote family planning
- Community problems with health and family planning services
- How services could be improved
- How much people would pay for improved health services

Interviews took place in the homes of influential community members, lasted about 2 hours, and were in the language of the people represented. They found, after recording and transcribing, that information collected in focused group interviews paralleled information collected by other means (Nkwi, 1992).

EXAMPLE 2.16

COMPARING RESULTS OF DATA ON THE SAME TOPIC
COLLECTED THROUGH FOCUS GROUPS AND SURVEYS

On the other hand, Ward compared focus group and survey data from three studies of voluntary sterilization in Guatemala, Honduras, and Zaire. He found that for 87% of the variables, results of focus group interviews were similar to those obtained through survey data, but that each provided useful additional information that the other source did not, demonstrating the importance of using both in good ethnographic research (Ward, Bertrand, & Brown, 1991).

The validity and reliability of group interview data depend on how much the researcher actually knows about the respondents and the contexts within which they live, and what the relationship between the researcher and the focus group members is at any point in time. They offer the advantages of gathering large amounts of text data in a short period of time and can be very useful in helping researchers to learn local vernacular and styles of communication and to gather different opinions about a topic. However, it is always important to remember that in ethnographic research, focused group interviews constitute only one set of tools in the ethnographer's toolkit. Focus groups alone are not sufficient to meet criteria of validity and reliability in ethnographic research. They must be accompanied by other forms of data collection and should be thought of as supplementing rather than replacing in-depth individual interviews, observations, elicitation techniques, and survey methods.

MANAGEMENT AND ANALYSIS OF FOCUSED GROUP INTERVIEW DATA

Group interview data are fundamentally qualitative. Most often, they consist of transcriptions of recorded group discussions and/or fieldnotes of observed group discussions in either formal or informal settings. These data are text data and are generally handled in the same way as other text data. A formal coding system should be developed and applied to the data if one or more of the following three circumstances prevail: if the number of interviews is large enough (more than 20 group interviews); if the interviews are long enough to warrant full-scale computerized coding (more than 15 pages); or if the research team decides that focused group interviews will continue, thus expanding the sample over time. In general, a database of more than 20 interviews, or more than 100 pages of text, warrants the creation of a coding system.

Cross Reference:
See Book 5, Chapters 4, 5, and 6, for more detailed information on coding

The creation of a formal coding system, and some examples of how it is used in computerized text management programs, can be found in Book 5. The coding system reflects the major questions and categories of interest in the research. Most often, it will begin with the core questions that frame the focused group interview, because each of these carefully thought out questions itemizes one critical component of the subject being studied. The coding system is then elaborated, based on the content of the interviews.

If the number of focused group interviews is smaller, the researchers may wish to reorganize all of the responses to each question in a single file. This can be done easily and rapidly using a standard word processing program. Researchers can then screen each file, searching for "classes of responses" and variations within each "class." Classes and variations are then described, the implications of variations within classes considered, and overall results summarized.

EXAMPLE 2.17

ANALYSIS OF FOCUS GROUP DATA ON WOMEN'S
REPRODUCTIVE HEALTH AND VIRGINITY IN MAURITIUS

In Mauritius, six focused group discussion sessions were held on reproductive health. One of the key questions asked how young, unmarried women felt about keeping their virginity. All of the responses to this question were summarized in a single file labeled "virginity." Schensul then reviewed the responses and organized them into subcategories reflecting "valuing virginity," "men's roles in preserving virginity," "male and female virginity," "changes in attitudes toward virginity," "procedures for evaluating the status of virginity," and so on. These subcategories were further analyzed for variations in response. The results were described and summarized for each "class," paying special attention to variations in response. Variations across all categories seemed to be related to changes in the status and importance of virginity. These changes were then discussed by the research team in the context of the changing economic status of women newly entering the workforce in this newly industrialized country.

◆━●━◆━●━◆

When completing a report, each source of data collected within a focused group setting should be analyzed separately. The results of one source of data should then be considered in relation to the others. This is referred to as **triangulation.** Triangulation is facilitated by the use of a matrix that summarizes the results obtained with each source of data. A matrix can summarize the results of each type of data collection by focus group, or it can summarize across all focus groups.

Definition: Triangulation is the corroboration of results from one kind of data by results obtained by collection of a different kind of data

Focus Group	Focused Group Data Collection Results		
	From Group Interviews	From Freelists	From Social Maps
1			
2			
3			
4			

A second matrix can summarize the results of data collected on the topic from focused group interviews in relation to other sources of data, such as key informant interviews, network analysis, participant observation, and so on. The process of comparing and contrasting responses and interpreting results is also referred to as triangulation. Results of focused group interviews can be incorporated into other materials for dissemination, or they can be reported separately.

Cross Reference: See Book 7 for more guidance on approaches to dissemination of ethnographic research results

EXAMPLE 2.18

PRESENTING THE RESULTS OF FOCUSED GROUP RESEARCH:
WHEN RESULTS ARE UNEXPECTED OR UNPOPULAR

In his study of knowledge about HIV/AIDS among Latinos, Elias Martinez attempted to select for focus group participation representatives of the population who were most at risk for contracting HIV/AIDS. His selection process was hampered both by the tight time line established for the project by the sponsoring organization, Boulder County AIDS Project (BCAP), and by the difficulties of recruiting people willing to talk about such a sensitive and culturally loaded topic—especially because many of the people most at risk were not legal residents of the United States and did not want to be identifiable.

The results of the focus groups showed that BCAP's intervention strategies were not reaching the target population at all. Print media were particularly ineffective; brochures were not used because they were placed in clinics whose doctors the target population mistrusted and felt abused by, and because they were not in Spanish. More useful modes of dissemination would have been radio or TV media, especially the Spanish-language "novellas," or soap operas, with which all Latinos were familiar. Furthermore, gender issues and practices complicated prevention; regardless of their age or educational level, women felt unable to resist male demands for unprotected sex or to combat a widespread belief among Latino men that males who adopt the "active" role in intercourse with other men, or who have sex with both men and women, cannot be homosexuals and therefore cannot contract what they thought of as the "gay" disease.

BCAP had specified that data be collected through the use of focus groups, but it soon became clear that members of the BCAP Board of Directors did not understand the limitations of focus group data. Martinez's first draft report was heavily criticized for its lack of "statistics." Board members wanted to know such things as the percentage of Latino migrant workers who used condoms to prevent HIV/AIDS compared to middle-class and professional Latinos, the percentage of Latinos overall who had read the BCAP brochures, and the number of people unable to read or understand English among the population. These figures were impossible to obtain using focus groups, although the report did cover well the series of hypotheses about the effectiveness, or lack thereof, of BCAP's educational interventions for Latinos, which the focus groups covered. Martinez rewrote the report to include as many numbers as he felt he legitimately could, describing the percentage of respondents within each opinion or informational category by group, but even that did not satisfy some members of BCAP. Some requested a larger and more systematic survey based upon the focus group results, but others ended the project feeling as though they had been cheated (Martinez, 1996).

ADVANTAGES, USES, AND LIMITATIONS
OF FOCUS GROUP INTERVIEWS

Focused group interviews can do the following:

- Provide access to a rich source of data on social norms, behaviors, opinions and attitudes, and the structural features of a group or community and cultural patterns. These can be used in conjunction with other sources of information to provide a well-rounded picture of the population, or to develop cultural intervention materials for use in behavioral change programs.
- Reveal the full range of variation in possible responses to questions for use in survey construction.
- Demonstrate styles of dialogue and debate among people who share or differ in important ways.
- Provide some evidence of likely quantitative variation in the target population in key independent and dependent variable domains.
- Provide the basis for generating important hypotheses that can be tested both qualitatively—through other focused group interviews—and quantitatively—in survey research designs based on focus group data.

These advantages not withstanding, focused group research has some limitations. As Martinez's study for BCAP illustrates, researchers must clearly explain the process and expected outcomes of focus group research, especially when there is the possibility that the users of the results are more familiar with, or place a higher value on, survey research. Furthermore, facilitators must be experienced and well-trained in the conduct of group investigation to produce good focus group data. Good focused group interviews cannot be conducted as if they were surveys. Most ethnographic group interviews, including focused groups, are semistructured or unstructured. They require that interviewers understand the conceptual framework of the study, know the breadth and scope of the information to be obtained, and use flexibility in finding appropriate ways of asking questions in the field. The quality and validity of the information may be influenced or hampered by the composition of the group and the interaction of the personalities within it. The logistics of recruiting and retaining formal focus group participation are complicated, especially when participants come from communities unaccustomed to group interview formats, or when they need supports such as baby-sitting, translation, and transportation. The process of conducting group interviews in culturally and linguistically diverse settings where translation must occur at multiple levels also raises important considerations with respect to validity and reliability of results obtained in focus groups—as, indeed, is the case for any research strategy.

Despite these caveats, most ethnographers use informal group interviews. Many ethnographers attend and participate in formal meetings that lend themselves to treatment as focus groups. Nowadays, ethnographers are turning increasingly often to more formal group interviews involving invited respondents who provide information for incentives of some kind. Careful advance thought and preparation can take good advantage of these unique opportunities to capture ethnographic data while also observing the ways in which differences in cultural beliefs, behaviors, and perceptions are negotiated by group members.

NOTES

1. A smaller group does not offer enough variation; in a larger group, some people may be too shy to speak.

2. A sampling frame consists of a set of criteria used to decide which kinds of individuals should be included in a sample.

3. This section draws heavily upon the work of Goetz and LeCompte (1984, pp. 208-231).

REFERENCES

Goetz, J. P., & Lecompte, M. D. (1984). *Ethnography and qualitative design in educational research.* New York: Academic Press.

Husaini, M. A., Satoto, M. D., & Karyadi, D. (1992). The use of RAP in the assessment of growth monitoring and promotion in North Sulawesi: Indonesia. In N. S. Scrimshaw & G. R. Gleason (Eds.), *Rapid assessment procedures: Qualitative methodologies for planning and evaluation of health-related programmes* (pp. 104-115). Boston: International Nutrition Foundation for Developing Countries.

Khan, M. E., Patel, B. C., & Hemlatha, R. S. (1990). *Use of focus groups in social and behavioral research—Some methodological issues.* Consultation on Epidemiological and Statistical Methods of Rapid Health Assessment, World Health Organization. E.M./CONS/R.A./90.18.

Krueger, R. A. (1988). *Focus groups: A practical guide for applied research.* Newbury Park, CA: Sage.

Krueger, R. A. (1998). *Focus group kit: Vol. 6. Analyzing and reporting focus group results.* Thousand Oaks, CA: Sage.

Martinez, E. L. (1996). *Report to the Boulder County AIDS Project.* Boulder, Colorado.

Merton, R. K. (1987). The focused interview and focus groups. *Public Opinion Quarterly, 51,* 550-566.

Morgan, D. L. (1988). *Successful focus groups.* Newbury Park, CA: Sage.

Nastasi, B. K., Schensul, J. J., deSilva, M. W. A., Varjas, K., Silva, K. T., Ratnayake, P., & Schensul, S. L. (1998-99). Community-based sexual risk prevention program for Sri Lankan youth: Influencing sexual-risk decision making. *International Quarterly of Community Health Education.*

Nkwi, P. (1992). *Report to the Population Action Program for the Improvement of Quality of Life in Rural Communities.* Yaounde, Cameroon: World Bank, African Population Advisory Council.

Schensul, J., Diaz, N., & Woolley, S. (1996). *Measuring activity expenditures of Puerto Rican children.* Paper presented at the second annual conference of the National Puerto Rican Studies Association, San Juan, PR.

Schensul, J., Torres, M., & Wetle, T. (1994). *The Latino Alzheimer's education curriculum.* Hartford, CT: Institute for Community Research.

Scrimshaw, S. (1992). Adaptation of anthropological methodologies to rapid assessment of nutrition and primary health care. In N. S. Scrimshaw & G. R. Gleason (Eds.), *Rapid assessment procedures: Qualitative methodologies for planning and evaluation of health-related programmes* (pp. 24-38). Boston: International Nutrition Foundation for Developing Countries.

Silva, K. T., Schensul, S., Schensul, J., Nastasi, B. K., de Silva, M. W. A., Sivayoganathan, C., Ratnayake, P., Wedisinghe, P., Lewis, J., Eisenberg, M., & Aponso, H. (1997). *Youth and sexual risk in Sri Lanka.* Phase 2 Research Report Series #3, Women and AIDS Program, ICRW. Washington, DC: International Center for Research on Women.

Spradley, J. P. (1979). *The ethnographic interview.* New York: Holt, Rinehart & Winston.

Stewart, D. W., & Shamdasani, P. N. (1990). *Focus groups: Theory and practice.* Newbury Park, CA: Sage.

Trotter, R., II, & Schensul, J. (1998). Research methods in applied anthropology. In H. R. Bernard (Ed.), *Handbook of methods in cultural anthropology.* Walnut Creek, CA: AltaMira.

Ward, V. M., Bertrand, J. T., & Brown, L. F. (1991). The comparability of focus group and survey results. *Evaluation Review, 15,* 226-283.

Watters, J. K., & Biernacki, P. (1989). Targeted sampling: Options for the study of hidden populations. *Social Problems, 36*(4), 17-18.

SUGGESTED RESOURCES

Morgan, D. L., & Krueger, R. A. (1997). *The focus group kit.* Thousand Oaks, CA: Sage.

> The six books in this series cover most aspects of conducting focus groups and using the results. Topics include planning, question development, moderating focus group discussions, involving community members in focus group interviews, and analysis and reporting of data. The kit is cross referenced and includes many examples. It does not cover informal group interviews or integration of focused group interview data with other data sources in ethnographic research.

Stewart, D. W., & Shamdasani, P. N. (1990). *Focus groups: Theory and practice.* Newbury Park, CA: Sage.

> This book covers most of the topics in the **Focus Group Kit** in a concise way with examples. One additional strength of this earlier monograph is the introduction, which provides a theoretical background to focus group interviewing.

Krueger, R. A. (1988). *Focus groups: A practical guide for applied research.* Newbury Park, CA: Sage.

> The topics covered in this book are similar to those in the preceding two. In addition, this earlier volume considers the wide variety of ways that focus group interviews can be used and contains an interesting chapter on contracting for focus groups from a consumer perspective.

Scrimshaw, N. S., & Gleason, G. R. (Eds.). (1992). *Rapid assessment procedures: Qualitative methodologies for planning and evaluation of health related programmes.* Boston: International Nutrition Foundation for Developing Countries.

> This interesting collection of articles promotes the advantages of rapid ethnographic assessment for enhancing culturally appropriate approaches to intervention in community settings around the world. Although it does not address focused group interviews directly, most chapters give examples of how focus groups can be used in RAPs and rapid rural appraisement.

3 ━●━●━●━

ELICITATION TECHNIQUES FOR CULTURAL DOMAIN ANALYSIS

Stephen P. Borgatti

INTRODUCTION

The techniques described in this chapter are used to understand **cultural domains** (Lounsbury, 1964; Spradley, 1979; Weller & Romney, 1988). A cultural domain is a mental category, such as "animals" or "illnesses." It is a set of items that are all alike in some important way. Humans in all cultures classify the world around them into domains, and the way they do this affects the way they interact with the world. Not all cultures classify things the same way. For example, English speakers recognize a category called "shrubs," which is different from "trees" and "grasses." But many other cultures do not recognize the "shrub" category at all: They divide up the plant kingdom differently. Even when cultures have the same domains, the contents may be somewhat different. For example, many cultures have a domain called "illnesses," but these cultures

Definition: A cultural domain is a set of items or things that are all of the same type or category

AUTHOR'S NOTE: I am grateful to H. Russell Bernard, Pertti Pelto, A. Kimball Romney, and Gery Ryan for helping to shape my views on cultural domain analysis, which is not to say that they necessarily agree with anything I have written. I am also grateful to Mark Fleisher and to John Gatewood for giving me permission to use their data to illustrate concepts. Finally, I thank Jay Schensul and Marki LeCompte for their many comments on earlier drafts.

often include as illnesses things that most Americans would regard as imaginary, such as "evil eye," or things that Americans regard as symptoms, such as "stomach pains." Ethnographers often begin their studies by trying to identify and describe the cultural domains that are used by the people they are studying.

The techniques described in this chapter are used to (a) elicit the items in a cultural domain, (b) elicit the attributes and relations that structure the domain, and (c) measure the positions of the items in the domain structure. These techniques, which include freelists, pilesorts, triads, and multidimensional scaling, have been incorporated into a commercially available computer program called Anthropac (Borgatti, 1992).

DEFINING CULTURAL DOMAINS

There are several ways to define a cultural domain. A good starting point is the following definition: a set of items, all of which a group of people define as belonging to the same type. For example, "animals" is a cultural domain. The members of the domain of animals are all the animals that have been named, such as dogs, cats, horses, lions, tigers, and so on. But there is more to the idea than just a set of items of the same type. Implicit in the notion is also the idea that membership in the cultural domain is determined by more than the individual respondent—the domain exists "out there" in the language, in the culture, or in nature. Hence, the set of colors that a given individual likes to wear is not what we mean by a cultural domain.

Key point *One rule of thumb for distinguishing cultural domains from other lists is that cultural domains are about people's perceptions rather than people's preferences.* Hence, "my favorite foods" is not a cultural domain, but "things that are edible" is. Another way to put it is that cultural domains are about things "out there" in reality, so that, in principle, questions about the members of a domain have a right answer. Consider, for example, the cultural domain of animals. If asked whether a tiger is an animal, the respondent feels that she is discussing a fact about the world outside, not about herself. In contrast, if she is asked whether "vanilla" is one of her favorite ice cream flavors, the respondent feels that she is revealing more about herself than about vanilla ice cream. In this sense, cultural domains are experienced as outside the individual and shared across individuals.

The fact that cultural domains are shared across individuals does not mean that all members of a given population are in complete agreement on which items belong to a given cultural domain. The extent to which a cultural domain is actually shared in any given population is an empirical question—that is, a question that is open to testing.[1] Conversely, simple agreement about a set of items does not imply that the set is a cultural domain. If we ask 1,000 randomly sampled informants in our own culture about their 10 favorite foods and every one of them happens to give the same list, it is still not a cultural domain because personal preferences are not the kind of thing that *in principle* could be a cultural domain. In contrast, responses to the question, "What foods are preferred in your community?" *could* be a cultural domain.

Another aspect of cultural domains is that they have **internal structure**. That is, they are systems of items related by a web of relationships. For example, in the domain of animals, some animals are understood to eat other animals. The relation here is "eats," and every pair of animals can be evaluated to see if the first animal eats the second. Another relation applicable to animals, recognized by biologists at least, is "competes with."

A relation of particular importance that seems to be common to all cultural domains is the relation of similarity.

Definition: The internal structure of a cultural domain refers to the relationships that exist among the items or things in it

It appears that, for all cultural domains, respondents can readily indicate which pairs of items they consider similar, and which they consider dissimilar. Another relation that seems to apply to most domains is co-occurrence, as in which foods "go with" which others, or which animals live in the same habitats with which others.

Relations among things are a fundamental aspect of how humans think about the world. Lists of "universal" relations have been made by many researchers, including Casagrande and Hale (1967) and Spradley (1979). Spradley's list includes the following:

- Cause and effect (X causes Y, Y is the result of X)
- Inclusion (X is a kind of Y)
- Rationale (X is a reason for doing Y)
- Means-end (X is a way to accomplish Y)
- Sequence (X follows Y)
- Function (X is used for Y)
- Spatial (X is a part of Y; X is a place in Y)
- Attribution (X is a characteristic of Y)
- Location for action (X is a place for doing Y)

Most of these, however, are not relations among items in the same domain, but rather relate the items from one domain to the items in another domain. For example, *location for action* relates a place, such as "Madrid" with an activity, such as "bullfighting"; places and activities typically belong to different cognitive domains. Similarly, the cause of a given effect is not necessarily a member of the same cognitive domain as the effect. For instance, making love may result in getting AIDS, but most respondents think of love as belonging to the domain of "feelings/emotions" while AIDS is a member of the domain of "illnesses." In this chapter we concentrate on only those relations that relate items within a single cognitive domain.

Other largely universal relations are semantic relations among the *terms* used to label items in a cultural domain.

These are relations such as synonymy (same meaning) and antonymy (opposite meaning). For example, in the domain of illnesses, there is often more than one term for a given illness (such as a folk name and a medical term). Although the line separating relations among *terms* from relations among the items themselves may be difficult to draw, in principle, our interest here is in the relations among the items rather than among the terms we use to describe them.

An important class of relations among items is the kind that can be reduced to a single attribute. For example, in the domain of illnesses, some illnesses are seen as "more contagious" than other illnesses. This relation is based on a single property of each illness in the domain, which is how contagious it is. This is different from the relation of (perceived) similarity, which is indivisible. We cannot attach a similarity score to an individual item—it is always attached to a pair. For example, we can say that the similarity between "pneumonia" and "flu" is 8 on a scale of 1 to 10, but it doesn't make sense to assign a similarity score to just one of the illnesses by itself (as in, "The flu has a similarity score of 3"). In contrast, it does make sense to assign to an individual illness a contagion score: We don't have to do it in pairs. The difference between attributes of individual items and relations among pairs of items becomes more clear as we go along in this chapter.

In general, an attribute that makes sense for some items in a cultural domain will make sense for all items. In other words, if "sweetness" is a sensible attribute of fruit, then it is meaningful to ask "How sweet is _____?" of all fruit in the domain. If the attribute cannot be applied to all items, this is sometimes because not all of the items are at the same level of contrast, which in turn means that subdomains exist. For example, if the domain of "animals" contains the items "squirrel," "ant," and "mammal," informants will be confused if asked whether squirrels are faster than mammals. The real test for items of different levels of contrast,

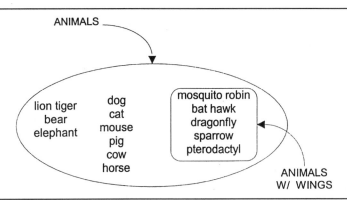

Figure 3.1.
Hierarchically
structured domain.

Definition:
Cover terms
are summary terms
encompassing
all the items in a
domain or
subdomain

however, is to look at the semantic "is a kind of" relation (Casagrande & Hale, 1967; Spradley, 1979). If any item in a domain is a kind of any other item in the domain (e.g., a squirrel is a kind of mammal), then you know that the latter item is actually a **cover term** (or a "gloss") for a subdomain.

Even if all of the items are of the same level of contrast, however, the inability to apply an attribute to all items is sufficient to suggest that the domain has a hierarchical taxonomic structure, and that the attribute belongs to items in one particular class. For example, the attribute "shape of wings" can be applied to some animals, but not to others. This means that the domain of animals contains at least two types—animals with wings and animals without—and within the set of those with wings, we can ask what shape the wings are (see Figure 3.1).

ELICITING CULTURAL DOMAINS USING FREELISTS

Definition:
The freelist
technique is used to
elicit the elements or
members of a
cultural domain

For domains that have a name or are easily described, the freelist technique is very simple: Just ask a set of informants to list all the members of the domain. For example, you might ask them to list all the names of illnesses that they can recall. If you do not know the name of a domain, you may have to elicit that first. For example, you can ask, "What

TABLE 3.1 Comparison of Freelist and Open-Ended Questions

Type of Question	Example	Objective
Freelist question	What illnesses are there?	Learn about the domain (e.g., develop list of named illnesses)
Survey open-ended	What illnesses have you had?	Learn about the respondent (e.g., obtain patient history)

is a mango?" and very likely you will get a response like "It's a kind of fruit." Then you can ask, "What other kinds of fruit are there?" Note that if a set of items does not have a name in a given culture, it is likely that it is not (yet) a domain in that culture. However, you can still obtain a list of related items by asking questions such as, "What else is there that is like a mango?"

At first glance, the freelist technique may appear to be the same as any open-ended question, such as "What illnesses have you had?" The difference is that freelisting is used to elicit cultural domains, and open-ended questions are used to elicit information about individual informants (see Table 3.1). In principle, the freelists from different respondents who belong to the same culture should be comparable and similar because the stimulus question is about something outside themselves and that they have in common with other members. In contrast, an open-ended question could easily generate only unique answers.

COLLECTING FREELIST DATA

Ordinarily, freelists are obtained as part of a semistructured interview, not an informal conversation. With literate informants, it is easiest to ask the respondents to write down all the items they can think of, one item per line, on a piece of paper. The exact same question is asked of the entire sample of respondents (see below for a discussion of sample size).

TABLE 3.2   Top 20 Animals Mentioned, Ordered by Frequency

Rank	Item Name	Frequency	Respondent %	Average Rank
1	Cat	13	93	4.85
2	Dog	13	93	3.62
3	Elephant	10	71	8.20
4	Zebra	9	64	11.11
5	Squirrel	8	57	12.88
6	Tiger	8	57	5.50
7	Cow	7	50	10.86
8	Fish	7	50	13.29
9	Bear	7	50	7.00
10	Whale	7	50	13.86
11	Deer	7	50	11.29
12	Monkey	7	50	10.00
13	Giraffe	6	43	12.00
14	Gorilla	6	43	14.67
15	Mouse	6	43	8.83
16	Snake	6	43	13.33
17	Lion	5	36	11.00
18	Antelope	5	36	11.00
19	Leopard	5	36	12.40
20	Turtle	5	36	7.80

We then count the number of times each item is mentioned and sort the items in order of decreasing frequency. For example, I asked 14 undergraduates at Boston College to list all the animals they could think of. On average, each person listed 21.6 animal terms. The top 20 terms are given in Table 3.2.

The number of informants needed to establish a cultural domain depends on the amount of cultural consensus in the population of interest—if every informant gives the exact same answers, you only need one—*but a conventional* **Key point** *rule of thumb is to obtain lists from a minimum of 30 lists.* One heuristic for determining whether it is necessary to interview more informants, recommended by Gery Ryan, is to compute the frequency count after obtaining 20 or so lists from randomly chosen informants, then repeat the count after 30 lists.[2] If the relative frequencies of the top items have not changed, this suggests that no more informants are needed. In contrast, if the relative frequencies have changed, this indicates that the structure has not yet stabilized, and you need more informants. This procedure works only if the respondents are being sampled at random from the population of interest. If, for example, the domain is illnesses and the first 20 respondents are all nurses, the method might indicate that no more respondents are needed. Yet if the results are intended to represent more than just nurses, more (non-nurse) respondents will be needed.

The frequency of items is usually interpreted in terms of their salience to informants. That is, items that are frequently mentioned are assumed to be highly salient to respondents, so that few forget to mention those items. Another aspect of salience, however, is how soon the respondent recalls the item. Items recalled first are assumed to be more salient than items recalled last. The second column from the right in Table 3.2 gives the average position or rank of each item on each individual's list. With sufficient respondents (more than used in Table 3.2), it is often the case that a strong negative correlation exists between the frequency of the items and their average rank, at least for the items mentioned by a majority of respondents. This means that the higher the probability that a respondent mentions an item, the more likely it is that he or she will mention it early. This supports the notion of salience as a latent variable that determines both whether an item is mentioned and when. In recognition that frequency and average rank are both reflections of the same underlying property (i.e., salience), some researchers like to combine the two into a single measure.[3]

Figure 3.2. Sorted
frequency of
items in a
freelisting of the
"bad words" domain.

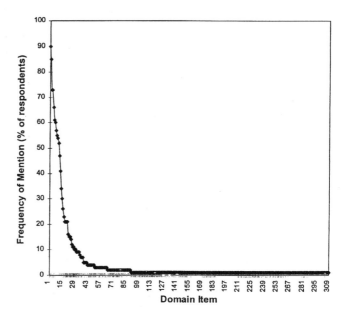

Once the freelists have been collected and tabulated, it usually becomes apparent that there are a few items that are mentioned by many respondents, and there are a huge number of items that are mentioned by just one person. For example, I collected freelist data on the domain of "bad words" from 92 undergraduate students at the University of South Carolina. A total of 309 distinct items were obtained, of which 219 (71%) were mentioned by only one person (see Figure 3.2). As discussed near the end of this section, domains seem to have a core/periphery sort of structure with no absolute boundaries. The more respondents you have, the longer the periphery (the right-hand tail in Figure 3.2) grows, though ever more slowly.

From a practical point of view, of course, it is usually necessary to determine a boundary for the domain one is studying.

Ways to Determine a Domain Boundary
- Include all items mentioned by more than one respondent.
- Look for a natural break or grouping.
- Define a boundary arbitrarily.

One natural approach is to count as members of the domain all items that are mentioned by more than one respondent. This is logical because cultural domains are shared, at least to some extent, and it is hard to argue that an item mentioned by just one person is shared. However, this approach usually does not cut down the number of items enough for further research. Another approach is to look for a natural break or "elbow" in the sorted list of frequencies.[4] This is most easily done by plotting the frequencies in what is known as a "scree plot" (see Figure 3.2). When such a break can be found, it is very convenient and may well reflect a real difference between the culturally shared items of the domain and the idiosyncratic items. But if no break is present, it is ultimately necessary to arbitrarily choose the top N items, where N is the largest number you can really handle in the remaining part of the study. In Figure 3.2, no really clear breaks are present, but there are three "mini-breaks" that one might consider. In the sorted list of words, they occur after the 20th, 26th, and 40th words.

One problem that must be dealt with before computing frequencies is the occurrence of synonyms, variant spellings, subdomain names, and the use of modifiers. For instance, in the "bad words" domain, some of the terms elicited were "whore," "ho," and "hore." It is likely that "whore" and "hore" are variant spellings of the same word and therefore pose no real dilemma. In contrast, "ho," which was used primarily by African American students, could conceivably have a somewhat different meaning. (There is always this potential when a word is used more often by one ethnic group than by others.) Similarly, in the domain of animals, the terms "aardvark" and "anteater" are synonymous for most people, but for some (including biologists), "anteater" refers to a general class of animals, of which the aardvark is just one. Whether they should be treated as synonyms or not will depend on the purposes of the study. It may be necessary, before continuing, to ask respondents whether "aardvark" means the same thing as "anteater."

Occasionally, respondents will fall into a response set in which they list a class of items separated by modifiers. For example, they may name "grizzly bear," "Kodiak bear," "black bear," and "brown bear." Obviously, these constitute subclasses of bear that are at a lower level of contrast than other terms in their lists. Occasionally, these kinds of items may lead respondents to generalize the principle to other items, so that they then list such items as "large dog," "small dog," and "hairless dog." In general, this is not a problem because these kinds of items will be mentioned by just one person, and so will be dropped from further consideration.

ANALYZING FREELIST DATA

Although the main purpose of the freelisting exercise is to obtain the membership list for a domain, the lists can also be used as ends in themselves. That is, several interesting analyses can be done with such lists.

Once we have a master list of all items mentioned, we can arrange the freelist data as a matrix in which the rows are respondents and the columns are items (see Table 3.3). The cells of the matrix can contain ones (if the respondent in a given row mentioned the item in a given column) or zeros (if the respondent did not mention that item). Taking column sums of the matrix would give us the item frequencies. Taking column averages would give us the proportion of respondents mentioning each item. Taking row sums would give us the number of items in each person's freelist.

TABLE 3.3 Portion of Respondent-by-Item Freelist Matrix

		Items							
		Cat	Dog	Elephant	Zebra	Squirrel	Tiger	Cow	Fish
	1	1	1	1	1	1	1	1	0
	2	1	1	1	1	1	0	0	0
	3	1	1	0	1	0	0	0	0
	4	1	1	1	0	1	0	1	1
Respondents	5	1	1	1	1	1	1	1	1
	6	1	1	1	1	1	1	1	1
	7	1	1	0	1	1	0	1	1
	8	1	1	1	1	1	1	1	1
	9	1	1	1	1	0	1	1	0
	10	1	1	1	1	1	1	1	1

The number of items in an individual's freelist is interesting in itself. Although perhaps confounded by such variables as respondent intelligence, motivation, and personality, it seems plausible that the number of items listed reflects a person's familiarity with the domain (Gatewood, 1984). For example, if we ask people to list all sociological theories of deviance they can think of, we should expect to find that professional sociologists have longer lists than most other people. Similarly, dog fanciers are likely to produce longer lists of dog breeds than ordinary people. Yet length of list is obviously not perfectly correlated with domain familiarity, because respondents who are relatively unfamiliar with a domain can produce impressively long lists of very unusual items—items with which other respondents would not agree.

To construct a better measure of domain familiarity (or "cultural domain competence"), we could weight the items in an individual freelist by the proportion of respondents who mention the item. Adding up the weights of the items in a respondent's freelist then gives a convenient measure

TABLE 3.4 Respondent-by-Item Freelist Matrix

	A	B	C	D
1	1	0	1	1
2	0	1	0	0
3	1	1	1	1
4	1	1	0	0
5	0	0	1	0
6	1	1	0	0

TABLE 3.5 Item-by-Item Matrix of Co-Occurrences
(Based on Table 3.4)

	A	B	C	D
A	4	3	2	2
B	3	4	1	1
C	2	1	3	2
D	2	1	2	2

of cultural competence. Respondents score high on this measure if they mention many high-frequency items and avoid mentioning low-frequency items.

Another way to analyze freelist data—now focusing on the items rather than the respondents—is to examine the co-occurrences among freelisted items. Table 3.4 gives an excerpt from a respondent-by-item freelist matrix. There are four items labeled A through D. Consider Items A and B. Each is mentioned by four respondents. Three respondents mention both of them. That is, A and B *co-occur* in three of the six freelists. By comparing every pair of items, we can construct the item-by-item matrix given in Table 3.5. This matrix can then be displayed via multidimensional scaling, as shown in Figure 3.3. In a multidimensional scaling map of this kind, two items are close together to the

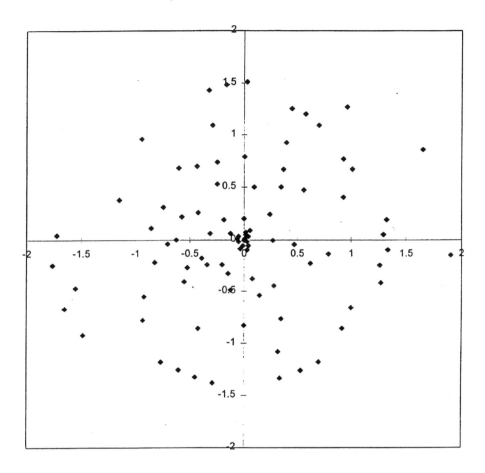

extent that many respondents mentioned *both* items. Items that are far apart on the map were rarely mentioned by the same respondents.

Typically, such maps will have a core/periphery structure in which the core members of the domain (i.e., the most frequently mentioned) will be at the center, with the rest of the items spreading away from the core and the most idiosyncratic items located on the far periphery. The effect is similar to a fried egg.[5]

There are a number of other ways to analyze freelist data. As Henley (1969) noticed, the order in which items are listed by individual respondents is not arbitrary. Typically,

Figure 3.3.
Multi-Dimensional Scaling (MDS) of 90 "bad words" based on their co-occurrence in freelists.
NOTE: Core items of the domain are found in the middle of the space. Items mentioned by only a few respondents are on the periphery.

respondents produce runs of similar items separated by visible pauses. Even if we do not record the timing, we can recover a great deal of information about the cognitive structuring of the domain by examining the relative position of items on the list. Two factors seem to affect position on the list. First, as mentioned earlier, the more central items tend to occur first. When we ask North Americans to list all animals, "cat" and "dog" tend to be at the top of each person's list, and they tend to be mentioned by everyone.

A second pattern is that related items tend to be mentioned near each other (i.e., the difference in their ranks is small). Hence, we can use the differences in ranks for each pair of items as a rough indicator of the cognitive similarity of the items. To do this, we construct a new person-by-item matrix in which the cells contain ranks rather than ones and zeros. For example, if respondent "Jim" listed item "Deer" as the seventh item on his freelist, then we would enter a "7" in the cell corresponding to his row and the deer column. If a second respondent named "Fred" did not mention an item at all, we enter a special code in Fred's column denoting a missing value (*not* a zero). Then, we compute correlations (or distances) among the columns of the matrix. The result is an item-by-item matrix indicating how similarly items are positioned in different people's lists, when they occur at all. This can then be displayed using multidimensional scaling. It should be noted, however, that if the primary interest of the study is to uncover similarities among the members of a domain, it is probably wise to use more direct methods, such as those outlined in the next section.

It should also be noted that although we reserve the term "freelisting" for the relatively formal elicitation task described here, the basic idea of asking informants for examples of a conceptual category is very useful even in informal interviews (Spradley, 1979). For example, in doing an ethnography of an academic department, we might find ourselves asking an informant, "You mentioned that there are a number of ways that graduate students can get into difficulty. Can you give me some examples?" Rather than eliciting all the members of the domain, the objective might be simply to elicit just one element, which then becomes the vehicle for further exploration.

It is also possible to reverse the question and ask the respondent if a given item belongs to the domain, and if not, why not. The negative examples help to elicit the characteristics that are shared by all members of the domain and that therefore might otherwise go unmentioned.

ELICITING DOMAIN STRUCTURE USING PILESORTS

The **pilesort** task is used primarily to elicit from respondents judgments of similarity among items in a cultural domain. It can also be used to elicit the attributes that people use to distinguish among the items. There are many variants of the pilesort technique. We begin with the *free pilesort*.

Definition: Pilesorts elicit judgments of similarity among items in a cultural domain

COLLECTING PILESORT DATA

The typical free pilesort technique begins with a set of index cards on which the name or short description of a domain item is written. For example, for the cultural domain of illnesses, we might have a set of 80 cards, one for each illness. For convenience, a unique ID number is written on the back of each card. The stack of cards is shuffled randomly and given to a respondent with the following instructions: "Here are a set of cards representing kinds of illnesses. I'd like you to sort them into piles according to how similar they are. You can make as many or as few piles as you like. Go!"

Figure 3.4.
Example of sorting
card for the domain
of "flowers."

ROSE

In some cases, it is better to do it in two steps. First, you ask the respondents to look at each card to see if they recognize the illness. Ask them to set aside any cards representing illnesses with which they are unfamiliar. Then, with the remaining cards, have them do the sorting exercise.

Sometimes, respondents object to having to put a given item into just one pile. They feel that the item fits equally well into two different piles. This is perfectly acceptable. In such cases, I simply take a blank card, write the name of the item on the card, and let them put one card in each pile. As discussed in a later section, putting items into more than one pile causes no problems for analyzing the data and may correspond better to the respondents' views. The only problem it creates is that it becomes more difficult later on to check whether the data were entered into databases correctly, since having an item appear in more than one pile is usually a sign that someone has mistyped an ID code.

Instead of writing names of items on cards, it is sometimes possible to sort pictures of the items (see Figure 3.4), or even the items themselves (e.g., when working with the folk domain of "bugs"). However, it is my belief that, for literate respondents, the written method is always best. Showing pictures or using the items themselves tends to bias the respondents toward sorting according to physical attributes such as size, color, and shape. For example, sorting pictures of fish yields sorts based on body shape and types of fins (Boster & Johnson, 1989). In contrast, sorting *names* of fish allows hidden attributes to affect the sorting (such as taste, where the fish is found, what it is used for, how it is caught, what it eats, how it behaves, etc.).

Normally, the pilesort exercise is repeated with at least 30 **Key point** *respondents,[6] although the number depends on the amount of variability in responses.* For example, if everyone in a society would give exactly the same answers, you would only need one respondent. But if there is a great deal of variability, you may need hundreds of sorts to get a good picture of the modal answers (i.e., the most common responses), and so that you can cut the data into demographic subgroups in order to see how different groups sort things differently.

ANALYZING PILESORT DATA

Pilesort data are tabulated and interpreted as follows. Every time a respondent places a given pair of items in the same pile together, we count that as a vote for the similarity of those two items (see Table 3.6). In the domain of animals, if all of the respondents place "coyote" and "wolf" in the same pile, we take that as evidence that these are highly similar items. In contrast, if no respondents put "salamander" and "moose" in the same pile, we understand that to mean that salamanders and moose are not very similar. We further assume that if an intermediate number of respondents put a pair of items in the same pile, this means that the pair are of intermediate similarity.

This interpretation of agreement as monotonically[7] related to similarity is not trivial and is not widely understood. It reflects the adoption of a set of simple process models for how respondents go about solving the pilesort task.

TABLE 3.6 Percentage of Respondents Placing Each Pair of Items in the Same Pile

	Frog	Salamander	Beaver	Raccoon	Rabbit	Mouse	Coyote	Deer	Moose
Frog	100	96	6	2	2	0	0	2	2
Salamander	96	100	4	0	0	2	0	0	0
Beaver	6	4	100	62	65	56	17	25	13
Raccoon	2	0	62	100	71	58	23	29	15
Rabbit	2	0	65	71	100	75	17	27	15
Mouse	0	2	56	58	75	100	17	15	10
Coyote	0	0	17	23	17	17	100	21	15
Deer	2	0	25	29	27	15	21	100	77
Moose	2	0	13	15	15	10	15	77	100

NOTE: Data collected by Sandy Anderson under the direction of John Gatewood.

*Process Models for Understanding
How People Do Pilesorts*

- They use a similarity metric or measure.
- They "bundle" or clump together items with similar attributes.

One such model is the metric model. Each respondent has the equivalent of a similarity metric in his or her head (e.g., he or she has a spatial map of the items in semantic space). However, the pilesort task essentially asks respondents to state, for each pair of items, whether the items are similar or not. Therefore, they must convert a continuous measure of similarity or distance into a yes/no judgment. If the similarity of the two items is very high, they place, with high probability, both items in the same pile. If the similarity is very low, they place the items, with high probability again, in different piles. If the similarity is intermediate, they essentially flip a coin (i.e., the probability of placing in the same pile is near 0.5). This process is repeated with each respondent, leading the highly similar items to be placed in the same pile most of the time and the dissimilar items to be placed in different piles most of the time. The items of intermediate similarity are placed together by approximately half of the respondents and placed in separate piles by the other half, resulting in intermediate similarity scores.

An alternative model, not inconsistent with the first one, is that people think of items as bundles of features or attributes. When asked to place items in piles, they place the ones that have mostly the same attributes in the same piles and place items with mostly different attributes in separate piles. Items that share some attributes and not others have intermediate probabilities of being placed together, and this results in intermediate proportions of respondents placing them in the same pile.

Both of these models are quite plausible. However, even if either or both are true, there is still a problem with how to interpret intermediate percentages. Just because intermediate similarity implies intermediate consensus does not mean that the converse is true, namely that intermediate consensus implies intermediate similarity. For example, suppose half the respondents clearly understand that shark and dolphin are very similar (because they are large ocean predators) and place them in the same pile, whereas the other half of the respondents are just as clear on the idea that shark and dolphin are quite dissimilar (because one is a fish and the other is a mammal). Under these conditions, 50% of respondents would place shark and dolphin in the same pile, but we would *not* want to interpret this as meaning that 100% of respondents believed shark and dolphin to be moderately similar. In other words, the measurement of similarity via aggregating pilesorts depends crucially on the assumption of underlying cultural consensus (Romney, Weller, & Batchelder, 1986). It is impossible to interpret the results of pilesorts if fundamentally different systems of classification are in use among different respondents.

To some extent, this same problem afflicts the interpretation of freelist data as well. Items that are mentioned by a moderate or small proportion of respondents are assumed to be peripheral to the domain. Yet this interpretation holds only if the definition of the domain is not contested by different groups of respondents. This could happen if we unwittingly mix respondents from very different cultures. For example, Chavez, McMullin, Martinez, Mishra, and Hubbell (1995) observed strong differences in freelisting responses by Mexicans, Salvadorans, Chicanos, European Americans, and European American physicians.

We can record the proportion of respondents placing each pair of items in the same pile using an item-by-item matrix, as shown in Table 3.6. This matrix can then be represented spatially via nonmetric multidimensional scaling, or analyzed via cluster analysis.[8] Figure 3.5 shows a multidimensional scaling of pilesort similarities among 30 crimes collected by students of Mark Fleisher.[9] In general, the purpose of such analyses would be to

- Reveal underlying perceptual dimensions that people use to distinguish among the items
- Detect clusters of items that share attributes or comprise subdomains

Let us discuss the former goal first. One way to uncover the attributes that structure a cultural domain is to ask respondents to name them as they do the pilesort.[10] One approach is to ask respondents to "think aloud" as they do the sort. This is useful information but should not be the only attack on this problem. Respondents can typically come up with dozens of attributes that distinguish among items, but it is not easy for them to tell you which ones are important. In addition, many of the attributes will be highly correlated with each other, if not directly synonymous, particularly as we look across respondents. It is also possible

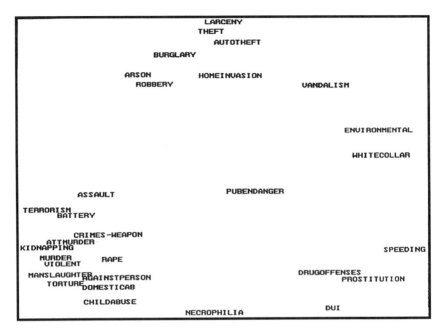

Figure 3.5.
Pilesort similarities among 30 crimes, represented by multidimensional scaling.

that respondents do not really know why they placed items into the piles that they did: When a researcher asks them to explain, they cannot directly examine their unconscious thought processes; instead, they go through a process of justifying and reconstructing what they must have done. For example, from a linguist's point of view, native speakers of a language are astonishingly good at constructing grammatically well-formed sentences, but they do not need to have conscious knowledge of grammar to do this.

In addition, it is possible that the research objectives may not require that we know how the respondent completes the sorting task, merely that we can predict the results accurately. In general, scientists build descriptions of reality (theories) that are expected to make accurate predictions but are not expected to be literally true, if only because these descriptions are not unique and are situated within human languages using only concepts understood by humans living at one small point in time. This is similar to the situation in artificial intelligence where if someone could construct a computer that could converse in English so well that it could not be distinguished from a human, we would be forced to grant that the machine understood English, even if the way it did so could not be shown to be the same as the way humans do it. What is common to both scientific theories and artificial intelligence is that we evaluate truth (success) in terms of the behavioral outcomes, not an absolute yardstick.

To discover the underlying perceptual dimensions that people use to distinguish among items in a cultural domain, we begin by compiling the attributes elicited directly from respondents. Then, we look at the multidimensional scaling (MDS) map to see if the items are arrayed in any kind of order that is apparent to us.[11] For example, in the crime data shown in Figure 3.5, it appears that as we move from right to left on the map, the crimes become increasingly serious. This suggests the possibility that respondents use the attribute "seriousness" to distinguish among crimes. Of course, the idea that the leftmost crimes are more serious than the rightmost crimes is based on the researcher's perceptions of the crimes, not the informants'. Furthermore, there are other attributes that might arrange the crimes in roughly the same order (such as violence). The first question to ask is whether respondents have the same view of the domain as the researchers.

To resolve this issue, we take all of the attributes, both those elicited from respondents[12] and those proposed by researchers, and administer a questionnaire to a (possibly new) sample of respondents, asking them to rate each item on each attribute. This way, we get the informants' views of where each item stands on each attribute. Then, we use a nonlinear multiple regression technique called PROFIT (Kruskal & Wish, 1978) to statistically relate the average ratings provided by respondents to the positions of the items on the map. Besides providing a statistical test of independence (to guard against the human ability to see patterns in everything), the PROFIT technique allows us to plot lines on the MDS map representing the attribute so that we can see in what direction the items increase in value on that attribute. Often, several attributes will line up in more or less the same direction. These are attributes that have different names but are highly correlated. The researcher might then explore whether they are all manifestations of a single underlying dimension of which respondents may or may not be aware.

Sometimes, MDS maps do not yield much in the way of interpretable dimensions. One way that this can happen occurs when the MDS map consists of a few dense clusters separated by wide-open space. This can be caused by the existence of sets of items that happen to be extremely similar on a number of attributes. Most often, however, it signals the presence of subdomains (which are like categorical attributes that dominate respondents' thinking). For example, a pilesort of a wide range of animals, including birds, land animals, and water animals will result in tight clumps in which all the representatives of each group are seen as so much more similar to each other than to other animals that no internal differentiation can be seen. An example is given in Figure 3.6. In such cases, it is necessary to run the MDS on each cluster separately. Then, within clusters, it may be that meaningful dimensions will emerge.

We may also be interested in comparing respondents' views of the structure of a domain. One way to think about the pilesort data for a single respondent is as the answers to a list of yes/no questions corresponding to each pair of items. For example, if there are N items in the domain, there are $N(N-1)/2$ pairs of items, and for each pair, the respondent has put them either in the same pile (call that a "yes") or in a different pile (call that a "no"). Each respondent's

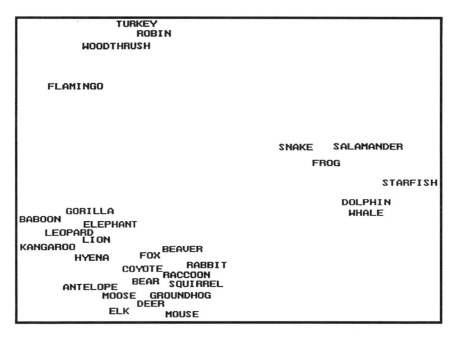

Figure 3.6. MDS of 30 animals, based on pilesort data collected by Sandy Anderson and John Gatewood. NOTE: The lower left cluster has been artifically spread out to avoid having labels right on top of each other.

view can thus be represented as a string of ones ("yes's") and zeros ("no's"). We can then, in principle, compare two respondents' views by correlating these strings.

However, there are problems caused by the fact that some people create more piles than others. This is known as the "lumper/splitter" problem. For example, suppose two respondents have identical views of what goes with what. But one respondent makes many piles to reflect even the finest distinctions (he's a "splitter"), whereas the other makes just a few piles, reflecting only the broadest distinctions (she's a "lumper"). Correlating their strings would yield very small correlations, even though, in reality, they have identical views. Another problem is that the strings of two splitters can be fairly highly correlated, even when they disagree a great deal, because both say "no" so often (i.e., most pairs of items are *not* placed in the same pile together). Some analytical ways to ameliorate the problem have been devised, but they are beyond the scope of this chapter.

The best way to avoid the lumper/splitter problem is to force all respondents to make the same number of piles. One way to do this is to start by asking them to sort all the items into exactly two piles, such that all the items in one pile are more similar to each other than to the items in the other pile. Record the results. Then ask the respondents to make three piles, letting them rearrange the contents of the original piles as necessary.[13] The new results are then recorded. The process may be repeated as many times as desired. The data collected can then be analyzed separately at each level of splitting, or combined as follows. For each pair of items sorted by a given respondent, the researcher counts the number of different sorts in which the items were placed together. Optionally, the different sorts can be weighted by the number of piles, so that being placed together when there were only two piles does not count as much as being placed together when there were 10 piles. Either way, the result is a string of values (one for each pair of items) for every respondent, which can then be correlated with each other to determine which respondents had similar views.

A more sophisticated approach was proposed by Boster (1994). To preserve the freedom of a free pilesort while also controlling the lumper/splitter problem, he begins with a free pilesort. If the respondent makes N piles, the researcher then asks the respondent to split one of the piles, making $N + 1$ in total. He repeats this process as long as desired. He then returns to the original sort and asks the respondent to combine two piles so that there are $N - 1$ piles in total. This process is repeated until only two piles are left.

Both of these methods, which we can describe as *successive pilesorts*, yield very rich data, but they are time-consuming and can potentially require a lot of time to record the data. The respondent also has a long wait while data are recorded. In Boster's method, because piles are not rearranged at each step, it is possible to record the data in an extremely compact format without making the respondent wait at all. However, it requires extremely well-trained and alert interviewers to do it.

ELICITING CULTURAL DOMAIN STRUCTURE USING TRIADS

Definition: Triad tests are an alternative to pilesorts in which respondents are asked to identify similarities and differences among items in a domain by comparing them in groups of three at a time. Triad tests are best utilized when there are small numbers of items in a domain.

An alternative to pilesorts for measuring similarity is the triad test. Triads are used for the following:

- Very small domains (12 items or less)
- Testing hypotheses in which it is important that every respondent make an active judgment regarding the similarities among a certain set of items
- Getting people to define which attributes they use to distinguish among items

In a triads test, the items in a domain are presented to the respondent in groups of three. For each triple, the respondent must pick out the one he or she judges to be the most different. For example, one triple drawn from the domain of animals might be the following:

Dog   Seal   Shark

Picking any item is equivalent to voting for the similarity of the other two. Hence, choosing "dog" would indicate that "seal" and "shark" were similar, while choosing "shark" would indicate that "seal" and "dog" were similar. If all possible triples are presented, each pair of items will occur $N - 2$ times,[14] each time "against" a different item. If a pair of items is really similar, it will "win" each of those contests and will be voted most similar a total of $N - 2$ times. If the pair is extremely dissimilar, it will never win. For example, "oyster" and "elephant" might occur in the following triples:

Oyster	Elephant	Dog
Oyster	Elephant	Shrimp
Oyster	Elephant	Ostrich

In the first one, the respondent might choose "oyster" as the most different. In the second, the respondent might choose "elephant." In the third, the respondent might choose "oyster" again, and so on. Hence, the triad test in which every possible triple is presented will yield a similarity score for each pair of items that ranges from zero to $N - 2$, where N is the number of items. For example, if there are 10 items, then each pair will occur against all $10 - 2 = 8$ remaining items.

The problem with presenting all possible triples is that there are $N(N - 1)(N - 2)/6$ of them, which is a quantity that grows with the cube of the number of items. For example, if the domain has 30 items in it, the number of triples is $(30 \times 29 \times 28)/6$, which is 4,060, which is too many for an informant to respond to, even over a period of days. The solution is to take a manageable sample of triples. For example, out of the 4,060 triples, we might randomly select 200 for the respondent to work with. However, a random sample would allow some pairs of items to appear in several triples and others not to occur at all. The latter would be a real problem because the purpose of the task is to measure the perceived similarity between every pair of items.

The solution is to use a balanced incomplete block (BIB) design (Burton & Nerlove, 1976). In a BIB design, every pair of items occurs a fixed number of times. The number of times that the pair occurs is known as lambda (λ). In a complete design (where all possible triples occur), λ obviously equals $N - 2$, because each pair occurs against every other item in the domain. When λ equals 1, we have the smallest possible BIB design, where each pair of items occurs only once. For a domain with 30 items, a $\lambda = 1$ design would have only 435 triads—still a lot, but a considerable savings over 4,060.

In general, however, $\lambda = 1$ designs should be avoided, because the similarity of each pair of items will be completely determined by their relation to whichever item happens to turn up as the third item. For example, if "elephant" and "mouse" occur in this triple:

Mouse   Elephant   Rat

it is likely that they will be measured as not similar, because "elephant" is likely to be chosen as most different. But if they happen to occur in this triple:

Mouse   Elephant   Oyster

it is likely that they will be measured as similar. Thus, it is much better to have at least a $\lambda = 2$ design, where each pair of items occurs against two different third items. The only exception to this rule of thumb occurs when you give each respondent in a culturally homogeneous sample a completely different triad test based on the same set of items but containing different triples. For example, Respondent 1 might get "mouse" and "elephant" paired with "oyster," but Respondent 2 might get "mouse" and "elephant" paired with "dog." In a way, this is like taking a complete design and spreading it out across multiple respondents. This can work well, but it means that you cannot compare respondents' answers with each other to assess similarity of views, because each person was given a different questionnaire.

A nice feature of the triads task is that unlike the simple pilesort, it yields degrees of similarity for pairs of items for each respondent. In the simple pilesort, each respondent essentially gives a "yes, they are similar" or "no, they are not" vote. In the triads, the range of values obtained for each pair of items goes from zero to λ. Hence, for a $\lambda = 3$ design, each pair of items is assigned an ordinal similarity score of 0, 1, 2, or 3. This means that we can sensibly construct separate MDS maps for each respondent.[15]

One problem with triad tasks is that respondents often find them tiring and repetitive. They will swear that a certain triad has already occurred and will suspect that you are trying to see if they are responding consistently, which makes them nervous. Another problem is that respondents tend to become aware of their own thought processes as they proceed, and they start feeling uncomfortable about using varying criteria (which is unavoidable) to pick the item most different in each triple. This makes them feel that they are not doing a good job. *In general, triads are useful only for very small domains (12 items or less) or for testing hypotheses* (where it is important that every respondent make an active judgment regarding the similarities among a certain set of items).

Key point

ANALYZING TRIAD DATA

Perhaps the most interesting use of triads was by Romney and D'Andrade (1964), who used them to test two theories of cognition about American male kinship roles, such as grandfather, father, son, grandson, uncle, brother, nephew, and cousin. One theory, by Wallace and Atkins (1960), held that Americans use two attributes—generation and lineality—to distinguish among the roles, as shown in Table 3.7. In the table, *lineal* refers to kin who are either ancestors or descendants of the speaker, who, by convention, is labeled *ego*. The term *collineal* refers to nonlineal kin whose set of ancestors includes or is included by ego's set of ancestors. The term *ablineal* refers to all other blood relatives.

If the theory is true, in a triads test that included the triple

Grandfather   Grandson   Father

TABLE 3.7 Wallace and Atkins Model of American Kinship

Generation	Lineal	Collineal	Ablineal
2 generations above ego	Grandfather		
1 generation above ego	Father	Uncle	
Same as ego		Brother	Cousin
1 generation below ego	Son	Nephew	
2 generations below ego	Grandson		

Americans should choose "grandson" as the one most different because grandfather and father are the least different with respect to the two attributes in the model (all of the terms are lineal, differing only on generation, where "grandfather" and "father" are adjacent, but "grandson" is a step removed).

In contrast, Romney and D'Andrade propose a model with three attributes—generational distance (e.g., number of generations from the speaker, or ego); lineality (see above for definition); and reciprocal roles (e.g., roles defined in terms of each other, such as father and son, mother and daughter, or teacher and student)—as shown in Table 3.8. In the table, "direct" refers to kin that share the same ancestors as ego (but not necessarily descendants), and "collateral" refers to all others.

According to the Romney and D'Andrade model, when faced with the same triad given above, Americans should choose, with equal probability, either "grandson" or "father" as the item most different, and should never choose "grandfather." Given these predictions, it was a simple matter to test the theories by giving the triads to a sample of Americans and seeing which theory best predicted the actual answers on the triads test. Overall, the best theory turned out to be the Romney and D'Andrade model.

TABLE 3.8 Romney and D'Andrade Model of American Kinship

	Direct		Collateral	
	– Reciprocal	+ Reciprocal	– Reciprocal	+ Reciprocal
Generation ± 2	Grandson	Grandfather		
Generation ± 1	Son	Father	Uncle	Nephew
Generation 0	Brother		Cousin	

INFORMAL USE OF TRIADS

So far, I have described only the formal use of the triads task, which results in the generation of similarities among items. Another way to use triads is as a device to spark discussion of the underlying attributes that people use to distinguish among items in the domain. To do this, we present informants with a small random sample of triples, one at a time. For each triple, the informant is asked to explain in what ways each item is different from the other two. This is an extraordinarily effective way to elicit the attributes that people use to think about the domain. For example, consider this triple:

Cancer   Syphilis   Measles

This triple can elicit a number of perceived attributes of illnesses including seriousness ("cancer is fatal"), age of the afflicted ("measles is something that kids get"), morality ("you get syphilis from sleeping around too much"), contagiousness ("you can catch syphilis and measles from other people"), and so on. It is easy to see that only a handful of triples is required to elicit dozens and dozens of attributes.

CONCLUSION

I have presented three basic techniques for eliciting data concerning cultural domains. The freelist technique is used primarily to elicit the basic elements of the domain. The pilesort and triad tasks are used to elicit both similarities among the items and attributes that describe the items. In addition, I have touched on the use of multidimensional scaling to illustrate graphically the structure of the domain and to locate each item's position in that structure.

Implicit in these data collection and analysis techniques is the idea of the cultural domain as a system or network of items related by semantic relations, or families of linked meanings. Thus, a cultural domain has internal structure, and it is the position of items within this structure that distinguishes the items from each other and gives them their unique meanings. Viewing domains in this manner emphasizes their fundamental similarity to other systems, such as economies, societies, ecologies, machines, and brains. Consequently, I would suggest that to obtain additional tools for studying cultural domains, we should look to those disciplines that have explicitly conceptualized their objects of study as systems or networks. In particular, I would recommend the techniques of social network analysis, which are reviewed by Scott (1991).

NOTES

1. Some people use the term "cognitive domain" to refer to domains that are not necessarily shared. For example, a psychologist might make an in-depth study of one person's understanding of nature. Because no other respondents were studied, the psychologist might refer to the person's categories as cognitive domains rather than cultural domains. However, it is important to realize that, whether they are shared or not, cognitive domains have all of the same properties as cultural domains, including being experienced as outside the individual. In this sense, we can think of cognitive domains as the general category, and cultural domains as a member of that category.

2. Personal communication from Gery Ryan, a medical anthropologist at the University of Missouri, Columbia. Dr. Ryan is a past instructor at the NSF Summer Institute for Research Methods in Cultural Anthropology.

3. One such measure, Smith's S (Smith, 1993), is given in the rightmost column of Table 3.2. The measure is essentially a frequency count that is weighted inversely by the rank of the item in each list. In practice, Smith's S tends to be very highly correlated with simple frequency.

4. You can also use salience, as captured by Smith's S.

5. Although not an artifact, exactly, of the column sums of the matrix (i.e., some items are mentioned more often than others), the core/periphery structure of co-occurrence matrices is made visible by not controlling for the sums. It is also useful to examine the pattern obtained by controlling for these sums. One way to do this is to simply compute Pearson correlations among the columns. Another way is to count both matches of the ones and the zeros.

6. The number 30 is merely a convention—a rule of thumb. More respondents is always more desirable but involves more time and expense.

7. This means that there is a one-to-one correspondence between the rank orders of the data. That is, the pair placed most often in the same pile is the most similar, the pair placed second-most often in the same pile is the second-most similar, and so on.

8. An excellent introduction to multidimensional scaling is provided by Kruskal and Wish (1978). For an introduction to cluster analysis, I recommend Everitt (1980).

9. The data were collected specifically for inclusion in this chapter by Jennifer Teeple, Dan Bakham, Shannon Sendzimmer, and Amanda Norbits. I am grateful for their help.

10. It is best to use a different sample of respondents for this purpose, or to wait until they have finished the sort and then ask them to discuss the reasons behind their choices. Otherwise, the discussion will influence their sorts. You can also have them sort the items twice: the first time without interference, the second time discussing the sort as they go. The results of both sorts can be recorded, analyzed, and compared.

11. It is important to remember that because the axes of MDS pictures are arbitrary, dimensions can run along any angle, not just horizontal or vertical.

12. The attributes may be elicited as part of the pilesort exercise, or by showing the MDS map to informants and asking them to interpret it.

13. An alternative here is to ask them to divide each pile in two. This is repeated as often as desired.

14. Again, N is the number of items in the domain.

15. The same was true for the successive pilesort techniques described earlier.

REFERENCES

Borgatti, S. P. (1992). *ANTHROPAC 4.0*. Columbia, SC: Analytic Technologies.
Boster, J. S. (1994, June). The successive pilesort. *CAM: Cultural Anthropology Methods Journal, 6*, 11-12.

Boster, J. S., & Johnson, J. C. (1989). Form or function: A comparison of expert and novice judgments of similarity among fish. *American Anthropologist, 91,* 866-889.

Burton, M. L., & Nerlove, S. B. (1976). Balanced designs for triads tests: Two examples from English. *Social Science Research, 5,* 247-267.

Casagrande, J. B., & Hale, K. L. (1967). Semantic relations in Papago folk-definitions. In D. Hymes & W. E. Bittle (Eds.), *Studies in southwestern ethnolinguistics* (pp. 165-196). The Hague, The Netherlands: Mouton.

Chavez, L. R., McMullin, J. M., Martinez, R. G., Mishra, S. I., & Hubbell, F. A. (1995). Structure and meaning in models of breast and cervical cancer risk factors: A comparison of perceptions among Latinas, Anglo women and physicians. *Medical Anthropological Quarterly, 9,* 40-74.

Everitt, B. (1980). *Cluster analysis.* New York: Halsted.

Gatewood, J. (1984). Familiarity, vocabulary size, and recognition ability in four semantic domains. *American Ethnologist, 11,* 507-527.

Henley, N. M. (1969). A psychological study of the semantics of animal terms. *Journal of Verbal Learning and Verbal Behavior, 8,* 176-184.

Kruskal, J. B., & Wish, M. (1978). *Multidimensional scaling.* Beverly Hills, CA: Sage.

Lounsbury, F. (1964). The structural analysis of kinship semantics. In H. G. Lunt (Ed.), *Proceedings of the Ninth International Congress of Linguists* (pp. 73-93). The Hague, The Netherlands: Mouton.

Romney, A. K., & D'Andrade, R. G. (1964). Cognitive aspects of English kin terms. *American Anthropologist, 66,* 146-170.

Romney, A. K., Weller, S. C., & Batchelder, W. H. (1986). Culture as consensus: A theory of cultural and informant accuracy. *American Anthropologist, 88,* 313-338.

Scott, J. (1991). *Social network analysis: A handbook.* London: Sage.

Smith, J. J. (1993). Using ANTHROPAC 3.5 and a spreadsheet to compute a free-list salience index. *Cultural Anthropology Methods Journal, 5,* 1-3.

Spradley, J. (1979). *The ethnographic interview.* New York: Holt, Rinehart & Winston.

Wallace, A. F. C., & Atkins, J. (1960). The meaning of kinship terms. *American Anthropologist, 62,* 58-80.

Weller, S. C., & Romney, A. K. (1988). *Systematic data collection.* Newbury Park, CA: Sage.

SUGGESTED RESOURCES

Borgatti, S. P. (1992). *ANTHROPAC 4.0.* Columbia, SC: Analytic Technologies.

Anthropac is a menu-driven computer program for cultural domain analysis. The program's capabilities include all of the techniques discussed in this chapter. More information is available on the Internet at http://www.analytictech.com.

Kruskal, J. B., & Wish, M. (1978). *Multidimensional scaling.* Beverly Hills, CA: Sage.

This is perhaps the clearest book available on the mathematics and interpretation of multidimensional scaling.

Romney, A. K., Weller, S. C., & Batchelder, W. H. (1986). Culture as consensus: A theory of cultural and informant accuracy. *American Anthropologist, 88,* 313-338.

This is a brilliant paper on the theory of consensus analysis—a seminal article in the field.

Scott, J. (1991). *Social network analysis: A handbook.* London: Sage.

Scott's book is a popular introduction to the techniques of social network analysis. It discusses everything from data management techniques to advanced analytical methods.

Spradley, J. (1979). *The ethnographic interview.* New York: Holt, Rinehart & Winston.

Spradley's book is perhaps the definitive book on interviewing technique in the context of cultural domain analysis. It is extremely well-written and has many examples.

INDEX

ABOUT THE AUTHORS, ARTISTS, AND EDITORS

Jean J. Schensul is a medical/educational anthropologist. After completing her M.A. and Ph.D. at the University of Minnesota, she conducted intervention research in education at the Institute for Juvenile Research and Center for New Schools in Chicago. She served as co-founder and research director of the Hispanic Health Council in Hartford for ten years, and, since 1987, has been founder and executive director of the Institute for Community Research, based in Hartford, Connecticut, and dedicated to community-based partnership research. She has extensive experience in the use of ethnographic and survey research methods in the United States, Latin America, Southeast Asia, China, and West Africa. Her substantive interests are diverse, reflecting the contributions of ethnography to health, education, the arts, and community development. She co-edited three special journal issues on applied research in education, and policy, and, with Don Stull, a book titled

Collaborative Research and Social Change: Applied Anthropology in Action, and has published on other topics including substance abuse prevention, AIDS, adolescent development, chronic health problems, and the arts and community building. She is the recipient of a number of National Institute of Health Research grants, immediate past president of the Society for Applied Anthropology, former president of the Council on Anthropology and Education, and recipient (with Stephen Schensul) of the Kimball Award for Public Policy Research in Anthropology. She is adjunct pro- fessor of anthropology at the University of Connecticut and Senior Fellow, Department of Psychology, Yale University.

Margaret D. LeCompte is Professor of Education and Sociology in the School of Education, University of Colorado at Boulder. After completing her MA and Ph.D. at the University of Chicago, she taught at the University of Houston and the University of Cincinnati, with visiting appointments at the University of North Dakota and the Universidad de Monterrey, Mexico. She also served as Executive Director for Research and Evaluation for the Houston public schools. In addition to many articles and book chapters, she co-wrote *Ethnography and Qualitative Design in Educational Research* and coedited the *Handbook of Qualitative Research in Education,* the first textbook and first handbook on ethnographic and qualitative methods in education. As a researcher, evaluator, and consultant to school districts, museums and universities, she has published studies of dropouts, artistic and gifted students, school reform efforts, and the impact of strip mining on the social environment of rural communities. Fluent in Spanish, she is deeply interested in language education and the education of ethnic minority children. She served as a Peace Corps volunteer in the Somali Republic from 1965-1967.

Bonnie K. Natasi, Ph.D., is Associate Professor and Director of the Programs in School Psychology at the University at Albany, State University of New York. Formerly, she worked as a school psychologist in the New Orleans public schools. She has extensive experience in the use of videotape and audiotape for data collection and analysis. Her research and applied interests include the role of culture, school, and family in the promotion of mental health. She consults nationally and internationally with schools and communities regarding the development and evaluation of primary prevention programs. She coauthored a book titled *School Interventions for Children of Alcoholics*. She is Associate Editor of *School Psychology Review* and currently serves on the editorial boards of *Journal of School Psychology* and *Journal of Educational Psychology*.

Stephen P. Borgatti is Associate Professor of Organization Studies at the Carroll Graduate School of Management, Boston College. He earned his B.A. in anthropology from Cornell University and his Ph.D. in mathematical social science from the University of California, Irvine. His research interests include social networks, semantic structures, and biological perspectives on economic systems. Among his publications are the following: *Reasoning With Numbers* (with W. P. Handwerker), ANTHROPAC 4.0 software, and (with M. G. Everett and L. C. Freeman) UCINET IV software. He is currently studying the adoption of organic farming in Finland and the social structure of the wine industry.

Ed Johnetta Miller is a weaver/silk painter/gallery curator/ quilter and Master Teaching Artist. Her work has appeared in the *New York Times* and *FiberArts Magazine* and in the Renwick Gallery of the Smithsonian, American Crafts Museum, and Wadsworth Atheneum. She is the Director of OPUS, Inc., Co-Director of the Hartford Artisans Center, and consultant to Aid to Artisans, Ghana. She teaches workshops on weaving, silk painting, and quilting to children and adults throughout the United States.

Graciela Quiñones Rodriguez is a folk artist, carving *higueras* (gourds) and working in clay, wood, and lithographs with symbols and icons derived from Taino and other indigenous art forms. She builds *cuatros, tiples,* and other Puerto Rican folk instruments guided by the inspiration of her grandfather Lile and her uncle Nando who first introduced her to Puerto Rican cultural history and Taino culture and motifs. Her work has been exhibited in major galleries and universities thoughout Connecticut, at the Bridgeport Public Library, and at the Smithsonian Institute.